THE THINKING TEACHER'S BODY

A Practical Guide to Teacher Well-Being, Vocal Health, and Development

HARRIET ANDERSON

A Note to the Reader

This book is not intended to be a substitute for medical diagnosis and treatment. If you are in any doubt as to the suitability of any of its contents for you, please consult a medical doctor or other professional health care provider. The author shall not be held responsible for any injury, loss or damage suffered as a result of reliance on any of this book's contents or any errors or omissions therein.

ISBN 978-1-32-032442-7

© Harriet Anderson, 2015

First Edition

The author asserts the moral right under the Copyright, Designs and Patents Act 1988 to be identified as the author of this work.
All rights reserved. No part of this publication may be reproduced, stored in a retrieval system, or transmitted, in any form or by any means without the prior written consent of the author, nor be otherwise circulated in any form of binding or cover other than that in which it is published and without a similar condition being imposed on the subsequent purchaser.

Harriet Anderson (Ph.D., MSTAT) is a teacher of the Alexander Technique and currently teaches in Brighton & Hove (England) and Vienna (Austria). She started her teaching life in academia. After graduating from Cambridge University she obtained her Ph.D. from University College London. She went on to do further original research on aspects of women's history and writing and published widely, including a full-length book with Yale University Press. She then joined the English Department at the University of Vienna, where she was for many years a lecturer. There her wide-ranging teaching included co-developing and running highly popular courses in spoken communication skills for trainee secondary school teachers, amongst others. In those courses she incorporated elements of body and voice work inspired by the Alexander Technique, of which she has been a qualified teacher since 1999. Harriet Anderson has since taught many professional development workshops and seminars for teachers and regularly coaches teachers, lecturers, presenters and others in speaking professions. She is a teaching member of the Society of Teachers of the Alexander Technique and a former Chair of the Society of the F.M. Alexander Technique in Austria.

www.harrietanderson.com
www.alexandertechniquehove.org.uk

It is quite wonderful how much Harriet managed to change in me with very little theoretical input and many practical exercises. After her course I am much more grounded, lighter on my feet, more alert and simply happier. Even my colleagues have noticed.
Christa Schmid, teacher

The voice coaching I've had from Harriet Anderson has been very beneficial to me especially in my professional life, which involves a lot of speaking. It helps me to use my voice more efficiently and with greater ease.
Dr. Gunther Kaltenböck, senior lecturer at the University of Vienna

Harriet Anderson is an excellent Alexander Technique teacher whose 1-to-1 sessions are working wonders for my physical and mental well-being.
Helen Limer, teacher and coach

Harriet's wonderful voice and her special way of explaining exercises to us inspired me tremendously. I just felt so relaxed three minutes after entering her class. Highly recommended for anybody who feels stressed.
Isabella Überegger, teacher

Working with Harriet enabled me significantly to expand my vocal range and presentation skills. ... I credit her with the dramatic improvement in my public speaking performance which was apparent to my colleagues but, more importantly, to myself.
Michael Payne, researcher at the United Nations

TABLE OF CONTENTS

Acknowledgements

Introduction
    Why this Book? — 1
    A Demanding Profession — 2
    Communication Matters — 3
    About Using this Book — 4

1   **First Principles** — 6
    Body-Mind Unity — 6
    The Force of Habit — 9
    First Principles Summarised — 14

PART ONE: LOOKING AFTER YOURSELF IN THE CLASSROOM

2   **Your Physical Well-Being** — 16
    Active Resting — 16
    Your Body Map — 22
    Exploring the Basics — 23
    Centered Standing — 29
    Strength and Stability — 34
    Exploring Everyday Activities — 36

3   **Your Vocal Well-Being** — 45
    Your Body is your Instrument — 47
    Exploring the Basics — 49
    Exploring Producing Voiced Sound — 55
    Voice Care Routine — 71
    Troubleshooting — 73

4	**Your Emotional Well-Being**	78
	Understanding Stress and Anxiety	80
	Self-Defence gone Awry	81
	The Psycho-Physical Approach	82
	The Power of Pausing	86
	Getting another Perspective	88
	In Search of Tranquillity	93

PART TWO: MAKING MORE OF YOURSELF

5	**Developing Your Speaking Skills**	96
	Speaking and Habit	96
	Speaking and Cultural Values	97
	Changing Speech Habits	98
	Coming Back to Neutral: Your Jaw	101
	Coming Back to Neutral: Your Lips	104
	Coming Back to Neutral: Your Tongue	105
	Total Pattern Awareness	111
6	**Developing Your Listening Skills**	116
	How we Hear with the Ear	117
	Coming back to Auditory Neutral	118
	The Work of Alfred Tomatis	120
	The Mind's Ear	123
	Kinaesthetic Listening and Speaking	124
7	**Developing Your Performing Skills**	129
	A Note on Identity, Context and Culture	129
	Physical Elements of Performance	131
	Vocal Elements of Performance	140
	Speaking with the Whole Self	149
	Daily Warm-up Routine	150

Troubleshooting 151

PART THREE: FIRST PRINCIPLES RE-VISITED

8   Wider Classroom Applications   156
     The Value of Challenging Habits   156
     The Usefulness of Mistakes   160
     A Note on Concentration   164
     "What?" versus "How?"   167
     Fear, Fun and Learning   170
     The Thinking Learner's Body   173

9   The Alexander Technique   177
     Alexander's Story of Discovery   179
     Applications   182
     Finding an Alexander Technique Teacher   184

ACKNOWLEDGEMENTS

I owe a debt of gratitude to all those who have contributed in their various ways to this book. Particular thanks go to Patricia Häusler-Greenfield whose inspiration, support and attention to detail stretch over years and national boundaries. Warmest thanks to Deborah Birnie for her helpful comments and many kindnesses, Regina Nening-Dougan for her sensitive thoughtfulness, and to Mel Bird for being open to the outpourings of a complete stranger. Thanks also to Sally Wilkinson for converting the typescript into a book and to Esther Hollander for the illustrations.

Like many teachers I am a thieving magpie and steal from others. Paula Anglin, voice coach *extraordinaire*, and Alan Mars, Alexander Technique teacher and presentation skills coach, have both offered rich pickings. I thank them. All mistakes, muddles and misunderstandings are, of course, my own.

To be a teacher means, above all, to spend one's life learning from one's students. This book has its origins in my own teaching experiences, both as a teacher of the Alexander Technique and as a teacher at the English Department of the University of Vienna, where my teaching for many years included a speaking skills course primarily for future secondary school teachers. From my many students, clients and colleagues I have learnt much. And without the confidence and encouragement some gave me this book would never have been written.

INTRODUCTION

Enjoy your body. Use it every way you can. ... It's the greatest instrument you'll ever own. (Kurt Vonnegut)

Why this Book?
This book puts teachers' needs firmly in the foreground. Fundamentally, it aims to help teachers do what they do with more ease, effectiveness and enjoyment. Teaching is an immensely worthwhile profession, yet many teachers experience physical pain, vocal trouble, burn-out, or simply do not know how to make the most of themselves in the classroom. As a result, everyone involved suffers. Much of this malaise can be traced back to Western thought's centuries-old separation of the human being into mind and body. The mind is valued over the body, which has been relegated to a place of subservience. This division is often particularly acute in the world of education, which still tends to see teaching (and often also learning) as an exclusively intellectual matter. Much has been written about teaching methods and resources yet, significantly, the teacher's body, the most important teaching resource of all, has been largely overlooked. At best it merits (sparse) attention when teachers prove to be all too human and vulnerable to illness. This book puts the teacher's body back into the classroom and promotes the integrated teacher who teaches with both mind and body. By giving teachers the opportunity to explore how body and mind speak to each other, it also introduces them to useful skills which will help them flourish, to the benefit of all.

A Demanding Profession

Teaching frequently takes its toll on the teacher's health and well-being. A report by the Department for Education dated 30 April 2013 found that 55% of teachers in English state schools took sick leave in the academic year 2011/12, with an average of 8.1 sick days per teacher. Vocal problems are a common cause of sick days, with teachers eight times more likely to suffer voice-related health conditions than other professions. Newly qualified teachers are even more at risk, with about half suffering voice loss in the first year of teaching.[1] Days lost due to stress-related issues are also endemic in the teaching profession. In a report by the Association of Teachers and Lecturers of March 2012, about three-quarters of those surveyed believed that the stress of the job was having a negative impact on their health. Teachers' ill-health has serious consequences, not only for the teachers themselves, but also in terms of their pupils' well-being and learning, and in financial terms as cover is expensive. In 2008 the bill for cover for teachers off sick with voice-related issues alone came to 15 million pounds.[2] In addition, even if they do not take days off work, many teachers are run down and in physical discomfort and vocal trouble. Clearly, such teachers cannot teach well, whatever methods they may be using. Equally clearly, the better teachers can look after themselves physically, vocally and emotionally in the classroom (and outside it), the better they can look after the learning needs of their pupils. However, it appears that during their training future teachers are not being given the basic skills to deal with the demands their profession will make on them. This book aims to help fill that gap.

Introduction

Communication Matters

The relevance of body awareness goes far beyond the essential skill of self-care, however. Effective teaching is very largely about communication and the building of relationships, not about the transfer of skills and knowledge alone. We communicate with our whole selves, with our bodies as well as with words. How we stand, gesture, our facial expressions, voice quality, intonation, use of pace and pause – all of this and much more is what the greater part of our impact is made up of. Students will subconsciously respond to all this and mirror our communication back to us. And on a very pragmatic level it needs to be stressed that easy intelligibility and audibility are essential for all teachers. This means having conscious control over how we speak and use our voices. The more body skill we have, the more skilful at communicating we can become, and therefore the better we can teach. The teacher's body is an essential teaching tool and resource. When in what follows we consider the significance of the teacher's body in the classroom, we are, then, not concerned with specially devised body-orientated methodologies involving movement and "games", but with what communication necessarily always involves.

This is, however, not to downplay the central place of language in communication. Yet that, itself, involves the body. Language, speech and the body are inextricably entwined. We master speech with our bodies as well as with our minds. "A language well learnt is a language well embodied".[3] That language and the body are inextricably linked is borne out by common turns of phrase. We react to words with our whole selves, body as well as mind, heart as well as head. We say that words can hurt us and we really do feel physical discomfort when on the receiving end of a harsh comment. We say that words can soothe, and we really do feel calmer and more relaxed after receiving a kind remark. Revealingly, we also say that words can touch us, for indeed speech is analogous to physical touch. We move in response to words, we respond with our bodies as well as our minds, with our whole selves. To speak is to create interplay between your own and another's body-mind.[4] This is an insight of great importance for all those in speaking professions, including all teachers.

About Using this Book
The following chapters are both informative and practical. They include straightforward exposition and guided explorations. Each chapter presents ideas, information, and where relevant also some basic anatomy. The explorations, which you can do at home, are intended to illuminate the material in a practical way and to give you the opportunity to make your own discoveries and to practise and promote your own body-mind skills. They add an essential experiential dimension. As skill development is cumulative, I strongly advise you to do the explorations in the order presented, that is, to start with the fundamentals and then proceed.

After taking a look at the fundamental body-mind principles which will accompany us throughout the book, we move onto how to look after yourself in the classroom. This first part deals with the three main areas of teacher self-care and well-being – physical, vocal, emotional – and emphasises the importance of body and mind in all three aspects. The second part goes on to look at how you can make more of yourself by considering three essential areas of skill development: speaking, listening and performing skills. The third and final part re-visits the first

Introduction

principles and considers how they could be helpfully applied to further aspects of teaching. It also tells you more about the book's inspiration, namely the Alexander Technique, a highly regarded body-mind method.

This book is best studied in conjunction with lessons from a qualified Alexander Technique teacher. You can read how to find one in chapter nine. However, as you may not be able or willing to take lessons, I have written it to be read, understood, and interpreted without such guidance. Bear in mind that change does not follow a straight path. As with all such books, you might find that some chapters and explorations are, at the moment, more useful and make more sense to you than others. And what seems obscure at first reading might very well later become clearer in the light of further exploration, experience and reflection. Enjoy.

---

[1] See *Voice Care*, NUT Health and Safety Briefing, p.1. on www.teachers.org.uk, website of the National Union of Teachers of England and Wales

[2] See *Voice Care*, NUT Health and Safety Briefing, p.1, www.teachers.org.uk, based on a survey carried out by the Royal National Institute for the Deaf in 2008

[3] Alfred Tomatis, *The Conscious Ear. My Life of Transformation through Listening* (Station Hill Press, Barrytown NY, 1991), p.89, first published in French in 1977

[4] See Tomatis, op.cit., p.90

1

FIRST PRINCIPLES

Man's body and mind ... are exactly like a jerkin, and a jerkin's lining; rumple the one, you rumple the other.
(Laurence Sterne)

Body-Mind Unity
What are the self-care skills all teachers need to learn in order to avoid common teacher health problems such as voice loss, burn-out, and chronic backache? We are showered with advice about healthy living, but advice alone usually does not lead us to change our behaviour, and it certainly does not lead us to acquire new skills. And how on earth are we to gain more conscious control over our teaching performance and our gestures, facial expressions and so on, which to most of us seem to have a life of their own? We need tools to help us.

Lurking behind most of our thinking about ourselves, despite modern lip service to holistic thinking, is the body-mind dichotomy, namely the assumption that body and mind are separate parts. Since Descartes, the dominant model in Western thought is that of the mind largely detached from the body. The prevalent view of the teacher's mind as a disembodied entity and of teaching as a disembodied undertaking is an illustration of that. But more than that: our language reflects and perpetuates this division, as much of what you could read in the Introduction testifies. You read, for example, of the physical and intellectual aspects of communication, of teachers' physical and mental health, as if communication and health could be subdivided into two parts (physical on the one hand, mental or intellectual on the other) which have nothing to do with each other. We do not have commonly used words for the wholeness of the human being. Connected to this way of thinking is the fact that we tend to see the workings of our body as also unrelated to our own behaviour and therefore outside our own control. We say "I've got a stiff neck", not "I'm stiffening my neck". This then makes us blind to how what we do to ourselves impacts on how we function and how we feel. Adherence to the body-mind dualism makes us less aware of our selves and reinforces a sense of powerlessness.

However, if we recognise that body and mind are indivisible, we can open doors to change. Everything we do, whether obviously active (for example speaking, walking, typing, driving) or apparently more passive (for example listening, sitting, standing, watching) involves body and mind acting together, whether we are aware of this or not. We are embodied mind and thinking body; we are psycho-physical beings. We cannot switch on a computer (that is, perform a physical act which involves our muscles) without the brain issuing commands to the muscles (which involves the mind). Similarly, how we sit at the computer, whether slumped or easily upright and balanced, is also as much a mental as muscular matter. And indeed, whether we sit slumped or easily upright also have their emotional counterparts: a slump probably induces feelings of depression and torpor, whereas sitting easily upright is more likely to make us feel engaged and alert. This in turn has a corresponding effect on the quality of the work we produce. How we do what we do affects the results we get. Sitting at the computer, like every other act, involves the whole of us. We are whole beings: moving, breathing, thinking, dreaming, feeling beings. We cannot split ourselves up into separate parts.[1]

Exploration 1: Exploring the mind-muscle connection

1.1 For this exploration it is best if someone else slowly reads it aloud to you while you do it. If that is not possible, read this description first. Do not rush this exploration.

Step 1
Make sure you are sitting on a chair with a firm seat, preferably one which does not slope backwards. Put both feet firmly on the floor, and sit on your sitting bones on the base of your pelvis. Sit tall. Put your hands out in front of you, palms facing upwards, and close your eyes.

Step 2
Now imagine that a heavy telephone directory is slowly placed in your left hand. Pause and stay with that thought. Really imagine that weight.
Then imagine that a light helium balloon is tied around the first finger of your right hand. Again, pause and stay with that thought of lightness.

Step 3
Imagine that a second heavy telephone directory lands in your left hand. Pause.
Again imagine that a second light helium balloon is tied around the middle finger of your right hand. Pause.

Step 4
A third heavy telephone book lands in your left hand. Again stay with the thought.

> And a third light helium balloon is tied around the ring finger of your right hand. Stay with the thought.
>
> Now, keeping your arms where they are, open your eyes and look at your arms.
> Is your left arm lower than your right? Even if not, do you feel a difference in the tension between your two arms?

I have done this exploration with many groups over the years. People vary as to whether there is a visible difference between their two arms and if so, how great it is. But almost all notice a difference in tension; the left arm really does feel as though it is carrying more weight than the right. The mind has, then, a direct influence on our muscles and how they work. This is an important insight. It means that we can learn to use our thinking to effect beneficial change in our muscles and therefore improve how we move. And it might also mean, vice versa, that what we do with our muscles can influence our thinking. We have here a powerful tool for change, based on our intrinsic wholeness.

The Force of Habit

Once we recognise our intrinsic wholeness, we can understand that our potential for change lies in our own hands. We are no longer at the mercy of a body with a life of its own or of a mind which is divorced from other parts of ourselves. At the same time, we can also recognise that one of the major obstacles to change is the force of habit in our lives. For most of what we do is done by habit. We perform our daily activities in a habitual manner: we sit, stand, walk, eat, breathe, speak in habitual ways. We do not think about how we do what we do. We also frequently respond in habitual ways to the stimuli everyday life throws at us. Some of those habits will be necessary, appropriate, or even beneficial for us. Without habits we could not survive in our immensely complex world. Looking right, then left, then right again is certainly a good habitual response to the stimulus of wanting to get to the other side of a busy road. However, if you have grown up in London and want to cross the road while on holiday in Paris, you might discover that your habit of looking right, then left, then right again is no longer beneficial; in fact it is a recipe for an untimely demise. It is, then, advantageous to have the potential to reduce the element of habit and increase the element of choice in our responses to the ever-changing stimuli of everyday life should those habits stand in our way.

Exploration 2: Exploring habits
2.1 Which everyday actions have you performed in a habitual manner since getting up this morning? For example, do you have a habitual way of brushing your teeth, tying your shoes, doing your hair, holding your cutlery…?

2.2 Which actions have you performed with awareness since getting up this morning? And which have you performed with a mixture of awareness and habit, an example might be driving a car?

2.3 What choices have you made today? About what you wear, eat for breakfast, mode of transport to use…?

Exploration 3: Exploring changing habits
3.1 Would you say that in general you find it easy to change your way of doing things and enjoy experimenting with new ways?

3.2 How easy do you think it would be for you to perform everyday actions in a different way from usual? Try it out. For example, try holding your toothbrush in the other hand from usual. How does that feel? Do you have a different system now for brushing your teeth?

Does performing familiar actions in an unfamiliar way make you more aware of what you need to do to perform the activity. Does it make you more aware of your habits?

3.3 Clasp your hands without thinking about it. Notice which thumb lies on top – right or left? Probably the way you have your hands now feels comfortable and familiar. It will be your habitual way. Now clasp your hands the other way round so that the other thumb lies on top. How does that feel? Strange? Wrong? Did you find it easy to change your clasp?

3.4 Fold your arms in front of your chest, one arm over the other. Now fold them the other way round. Again, did you find that easy? Was it more difficult than changing your clasp?

If you found it more difficult, take the opportunity to explore what you needed to do in order to fold your arms in the unfamiliar way. Starting with your arms folded as you usually do, you probably first needed to stop and give yourself time to look at your arms, take in which arm was on top, and then think and slowly reorganise yourself with the other arm on top. And probably the most important thing was to stop, observe and think.

This ability to stop is the key to relinquishing unhelpful habits and to becoming aware of the choices we have. It means giving up what is familiar and venturing into the unknown. This is the essence of change. You can explore habit and saying "no" to habit, or more precisely, withholding consent to habit, in the following exploration.

Exploration 4: Exploring withholding consent to habit

4.1 You need at least one other person for this exploration; a group is ideal. Depending on the size of the group you also need one or more soft balls. It is important that everyone knows that the balls are really soft and cannot hurt anyone or damage light fittings, windows etc.

Stand in a circle. The rules of the game are that the ball is thrown randomly from one person to another. Each person can choose whether they catch or do not catch the ball. If they choose not to catch, they pick it up and throw it on. It is important that all players know that catching and not catching are of equal value.

How do the rules of the game make you feel? Do you sense any anxiety at the thought of a ball game? How do your muscles respond? Do you notice any tension anywhere? In your neck, shoulders, face, jaw, arms, buttocks?

While playing the game be aware of yourself and any muscular tension. How easy do you find it not to catch the ball? Do you notice any muscular twitch to catch even when you have decided not to? How does not catching make you feel?

After the game reflect with your partner or other players on what you discovered about yourself and observed in others. What part might our earlier experiences, expectations and beliefs regarding ball games play in this?

In the numerous workshops where I have played this game I invariably have to invite participants to experiment with not catching. It seems that the habit to catch is deeply engrained in almost all of us from our childhood and schooldays; catching is, after all, what we are supposed to do. However, often when participants choose not to catch it can be quite a revelation for them. Most feel it is rather weird, some notice an involuntary twitching as if their arms still want to catch, a few find it very difficult or even annoying or impolite. But for very many, the realisation that they have a choice and are allowed not to catch is enormously liberating and a huge relief. And almost all of these people then experience more pleasure in the game and feel more connected to themselves while playing it. For almost all, catching becomes easier and takes on a different quality when it is not the goal of the game and a habitual response. And that different quality of response leads to a different quality of movement which is visible to the outside observer and more pleasurable to watch.

Now all this emphasis on stopping and choosing might sound like the end to spontaneity and a recipe for self-consciousness and stiffness. Actually, the opposite is the case. Learning to stop responding to a stimulus in a habitual way frees us from those self-limiting knee-jerk reactions which get in our way. It liberates us from those habits, be they muscular, emotional or intellectual, which sap our energy. Instead, freeing ourselves from those unwanted habitual responses gives us energy. This is an important insight. Withholding consent to habit has nothing to do with self-repression, or with being slow, quiet, passive, and never displaying strong emotions. On the contrary, it is about saying "no" to those habits which prevent us from flourishing and being at our best. By learning to withhold consent to self-restricting habits, we can have more choices and expand our repertoire of ways of being. As teachers, this means that the focus shifts from asking "What shall I do?" to "How shall I be?". By considering that question, we can learn to make the most of ourselves in the classroom, bring a new creativity into our teaching, and teach with our whole undivided self to the benefit of both ourselves and our pupils.

First Principles Summarised

These first principles are largely based on some of the ideas and principles of the Alexander Technique, named after its originator Frederick Matthias Alexander. You can find out more about Alexander, his discoveries, and the method named after him in the final chapter.

The principles and their wide range of highly useful applications will become clearer in what follows. For the moment we can summarise the tenets which will run through this book thus:

- We are integrated beings. In every situation we act and react with every aspect of our being (mental, emotional, physical, spiritual), whether we are aware of this or not.

- We are creatures of habit. Habit is a force which can rule our lives and prevent us from living with more ease and making the most of ourselves.

- We can gain more constructive conscious control over ourselves and our responses by learning to withhold consent to unhelpful habits. This opens the door to positive change.

---

[1] See Pedro de Alcantara, *The Alexander Technique: A Skill for Life* (Crowood Press, Marlborough, 1999), pp.8-11

PART ONE

LOOKING AFTER YOURSELF IN THE CLASSROOM

We first make our habits, and then they make us.
(John Dryden)

2

YOUR PHYSICAL WELL-BEING

How use doth breed a habit in a man! (William Shakespeare)

Teaching is in many ways a challenging profession. Teachers are confronted by numerous and varied demands: from students and colleagues, frequently also from institutional authorities and central government. They spend a large part of their working lives constantly surrounded by other people, often in cramped and noisy environments. Many, at some time in their careers, will have to deal with unwilling learners and discipline issues. And daily lesson preparation, teaching, and marking can often feel like a relentless grind. Combine all that with the many hours spent sitting or standing and it is hardly surprising that many teachers suffer from backache, shoulder pain, migraines, poor posture, and a variety of other symptoms of excessive tension which, in turn, can hardly fail to have an impact on the quality of their teaching.

Learning to look after yourself in the classroom is, then, a priority for a happy and successful career. Building on our first principles, this chapter will introduce you to some of the basic body-mind skills you need.

Active Resting
This is altogether the best thing you can do for yourself. It has three main benefits:

Your Physical Well-Being

Repair: by giving optimum support to your back, it helps your spine to lengthen. The intervertebral fluid in your spine flows back into and plumps up the cushioning discs between your vertebrae (excellent for avoiding slipped discs). By letting the superficial sheet muscles of your back rest and inviting your deeper postural muscles to be more active muscle tone is redistributed, which leads to a release in habitually over-contracted muscles.

Preparation: time out for you to come to calm, reflect, and re-connect with yourself in preparation for whatever you need to do next.

Practice: time to practise consciously connecting mind and muscle, the key to long-term change. It helps you gain greater control of how you respond to the stimuli everyday life throws at you and more constructive conscious control over your habits.

In general it promotes inner calm and clarity in thought, and a sense of heightened awareness and well-being.

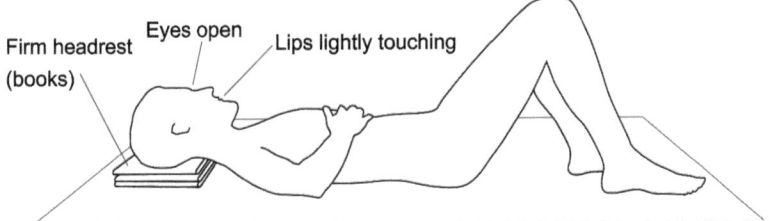

Figure 1: The active resting position

Exploration 5: Exploring active resting

5.1 This is the most useful exploration altogether. Even if you do no other exploration in this book, but do this one regularly, you will experience great benefit. The more often you can do it, the better. The rule of "little, but often" applies here. It is usually best to set aside a regular time each day. And even if you have only five minutes, still do it.

Getting into Position

The main thing to remember about getting into position is to do it slowly and with awareness.

Step 1

Place a small pile of paperback books (not cushions or pillows) on a firm surface, for example a rug or exercise mat on the floor. Don't use your bed. You might like to cover the books with a soft towel or something similar. It is better to use slim volumes so you can adjust the height easily.

Step 2

Get down on your hands and knees, turn around so that you are sitting with your feet on the floor, your legs bent, and your knees facing up towards the ceiling. Roll back slowly first onto one elbow, then onto the other, until your head is on the books. If your chin is pushing down on your throat, remove a book; if it is pointing up to the ceiling add a book. If in doubt, err on the side of having too many rather than too few books.

Step 3

Let your back rest on the floor (or however much of your back touches the floor easily), your knees bent and pointing up to the ceiling. The soles of your feet are on the floor. Put your hands on your rib cage or the big bones of your pelvis.

Your Physical Well-Being

Step 4
Try to keep your eyes open (so make sure there are no bright overhead lights). It is best to be aware of yourself and at the same time aware of the world outside you. The ability to embrace a unified field of attention, where you are not forced to choose between either the inner or the outer world but can unite the two, is extremely useful in everyday life and therefore worth practising in a protected situation such as this.

And then...
Be aware of contact with your support: Be aware of where you have contact with supporting surfaces (the floor, books): under your feet, your pelvis, your back, your shoulders, your upper arms, your head. Just observe; don't try to change anything. Now think of intensifying the contact by allowing yourself to release and soften onto the floor, like butter melting in a frying pan. Don't push, allow it to happen.

Allow lengthening and widening in your torso: Imagine your back has four corners: the top corner is under your head (contact to the books), bottom corner is under your tail bone (contact to the floor), the right and left corners are under your shoulder blades (which may or may not be touching the floor). Now allow these four points to swim gracefully away from each other, so you are getting longer and wider. Do not try to do any lengthening or widening, instead trust in your mental powers. Take your time; if there is any discomfort, stop.

Allow lengthening in your arms: Now allow your arms to lengthen and extend away from your breastbone, like two large wings ready to fly. At the same time keep the idea going of your four corners spreading away from each other.

Allow lengthening in your legs: At the same time allow your thighs to lengthen and extend away from your hip joints, while your heels are making good contact with the floor.

Keep breathing: Send your awareness to your breathing, allowing it to flow gently and rhythmically. Focus on the out-breath rather than the in-breath.

Do a body scan: Go around your body and notice any tension in a non-judgemental way – probably you already know what your favourite tension spots are. Clenched Jaw? Frowning forehead? Raised shoulders? Pinched buttocks? Tense thighs? Invite yourself to release if you notice some tension.

Rest awhile. If your thoughts roam, bring them gently back to your body; give yourself time to tune into a new way of being. Enjoy.

Getting Up
Do this slowly and with awareness.

Step 1
Look to one side (say to the left) and let your head follow your eyes.

Step 2
Stretch the opposite (in this case right) arm over your body, so that you roll over onto your (left) side. Pause.

Step 3
Keep rolling to get onto all fours. Pause.

Step 4
Slowly come into standing, pause, and re-enter your daily life.

Lying down and allowing your mind and muscles to speak to each other in this manner is immensely beneficial. However, it is important to be aware that you are not after relaxation in the sense of going floppy and mentally switching off or retreating into a self-enclosed inner world. What you are after is a release in those muscles which you habitually and unnecessarily overuse; you can invite that release by strengthening the mental messages you send to the muscles. It is, as the name says, active resting. This is important as your greater self-care goal is more control of reactions. Learning to control your habitual reactions of undue tension, which are both muscular and mental, is a good place to start.

The Principle of Compensation
But why, you might well ask, do so many of us have harmful habits of reaction? Why do we make ourselves shorter, tense our shoulders, clench our jaw? For many of us, these ways of dealing with external stimuli can have their origins in childhood. Boredom and fear at school, ill-fitting furniture, parental reprimands and injunctions combined with the child's eagerness to please, ridiculously heavy school bags, injuries and accidents, even misconceptions about how we are built and function, can all lead to unnecessary muscle tension and bring us out of alignment. We start to interfere with our easy functioning.

And then the principle of compensation kicks in. If one set of muscles stops doing the job that it is intended to do, others will compensate. This is the body's emergency mechanism to keep us going somehow, even if not in the best way nature intends. However, the principle of compensation comes at a price: impaired functioning and often discomfort or even pain. And unfortunately, compensatory muscle use usually remains with us, long after the original stimulus which sent us awry belongs to the past. Our habits of reaction become part of who we are. Undue muscle tension often feels "normal", "right" and "natural" precisely because it is so familiar and we usually go through our lives quite unaware of what is happening – until pain alerts us that something is amiss.

Your Body Map
We all have an internalised map of our own body. What we think we need to do in order to move is, more often than not, dictated by our map. Yet, also more often than not, that map is inaccurate and leads us astray. It can therefore be a source of harmful habits. As we move according to our map, it is important to draw an accurate inner map, so that it can be a help to us rather than a hindrance. However, having said that, in some cases we do not want to be a slave to our own anatomical and physiological knowledge. Sometimes, we need to use our great and wonderful powers of imagination and visualisation. Yet it is important that we know when we are using our imagination and that we do not confuse a helpful image with our anatomical reality. We need to imagine against the background of an accurate body map.

The first step in drawing an accurate and helpful body map is to get to know your own body first hand, that is: *Probe – Poke – Palpate.*[1]

> **Exploration 6: Exploring yourself**
> **6.1** With your fingertips explore your own skull. Start with your two forefingers under the front of your lower jaw bone and move out to either side, using more fingertips as you go along.
> What do you feel? The hardness of the bone, the sponginess of the tissue, the tautness of the skin? What is the precise shape of

that jaw bone? What happens as you go along? Where does the jaw meet the skull? Pay particular attention to this area. Probe. Poke. Try gently closing and opening your mouth by moving the lower jaw up and down. Be very aware that only the lower jaw moves up and down, not the so-called upper jaw which is part of the skull and cannot move independently of the whole skull. What do you feel happening under your fingers?

Continue along the base of the skull. Move your head around while keeping your fingertips on the base. What do you feel? Then with your palms feel the back of your skull, your own individual shape there (everyone is a little different). Then gently palpate your face, feeling for the bone of your eye sockets, your cheek bones, your nose.

6.2 Do similar explorations for your hands, feet, shoulder girdle, arms, legs.

It can be illuminating to sketch what your self-discovering hands tell you. This will not be an accurate anatomical drawing, but a representation of your own discoveries. You can continue to clarify your body map in the course of the following sections of this chapter and also in following chapters.

What You Need to Know: The Basics

Your Spine: Your spine is your central support system. It is long, thick, and at places deep inside your body. It should not be completely straight; its natural curves give it strength. It extends from your coccyx, right up to the level of your ears. Note that it might be longer than you think it is; it does not stop at the big neck vertebra at the collar of your shirt which often sticks out, but extends beyond that up to about the level of your ears. The weight-bearing part is the front, not the back (that houses the nerves). The bony, poky bits (spinal processes) you can feel with your fingers are not weight-bearing. The spine and the small, deep postural muscles attached to it are intended to give you support and keep you upright; this is not the job of the big, superficial sheet muscles of your back, which are there for movement. You can see the deep postural muscles (figure 2) and the superficial sheet muscles (figure 3) in these beautiful copperplate engravings by the eighteenth-century anatomist Bernard Siegfried Albinus.[2]

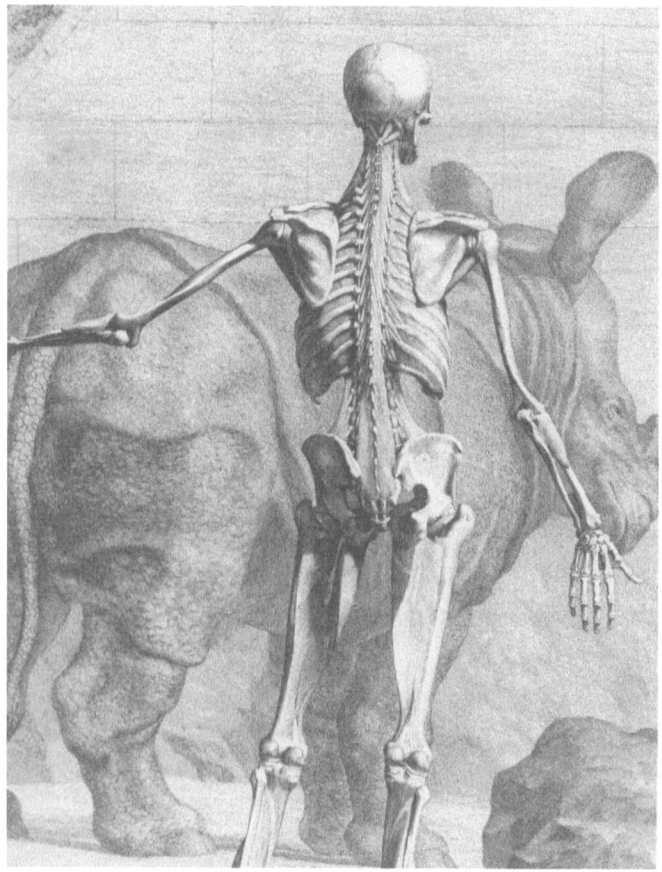

Figure 2: The deep postural muscles

Your Physical Well-Being

Figure 3: The superficial sheet muscles

When your body is well-aligned, weight will drop down through the weight-bearing front part of the spine, through the hip, knee and ankle joints into the arch of the foot and on into the ground. Understanding this, and learning to move accordingly, can liberate you from back pain.

Your head-neck-back relationship: The top vertebra of your spine which supports your skull is called the atlas, named after the Titan Atlas who, according to ancient mythology, held up the celestial spheres. The joint where your skull and spine meet is called the atlanto-occipital joint (your occiput is your skull) and is roughly level with your ears. It is not in the centre of your skull, but further back. This means there is more of your skull forwards of the joint than behind it. Your head is heavy (about 5 kilos/10 pounds) and should balance, beautifully poised, on the top of your spine at the atlanto-occipital joint. You might like to think of the delicate balancing act of one large boulder poised on top of another.

This balancing act is accomplished by the small, deep muscles at the back of your neck (see figure 2) exerting just the right amount of tension, but no more, to keep your head poised and balanced. As there is more of your skull forwards of the atlanto-occipital joint than behind, that extra weight needs to be counteracted by the finely-tuned action of the small, deep neck muscles to prevent your head dropping down onto the chest. This balance is crucially important.

However, it is easy to disturb it by overly tightening the neck muscles, which then pull the back of the head back and down. As the head is heavy and the ability of the spine to bear weight has been impaired by the loss of head balance and alignment, that weight compresses the spine, leading to a downward pull in the whole body (commonly called a slump). Alternatively, a back and downward pull of the head leads, in compensation, to what is often called a "military posture": the shoulders are pulled back to thrust out the chest but narrowing the upper back, the lower back is arched, the knees are locked back (see figure 4). Both these responses to loss of head balance are a frequent cause of lower back pain and both lead to a feeling of effortful standing and moving. They also lead to a loss in stature. Re-establishing head balance is an essential precondition to re-establishing total intrinsic functioning and therefore easier movement.

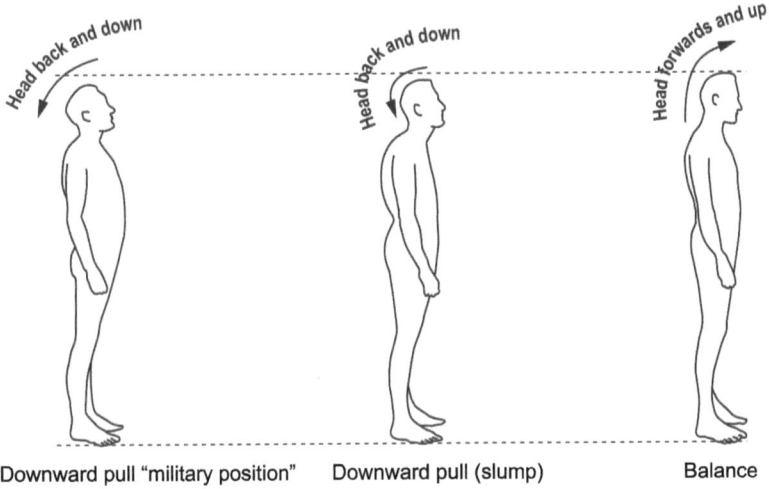

Figure 4: How head balance affects posture

Your Torso: You can think of your torso as a cylinder. At the base is your pelvis which at the bottom is shaped like the runners of a rocking-chair giving you a lot of stability and movement while seated. These areas are your sitting (or sit) bones. Note that they are not bones attached to the pelvis, but part of the pelvis itself.

Exploration 7: Exploring your sitting bones
7.1 Sit on a reasonably firm surface, slip your hand underneath one buttock and wriggle around. You will feel a hard knobbly bit. That is a sitting bone; you have another on the other side. As the name suggests, these are the bony areas you should sit on.

7.2 Try rocking forwards and backwards on these rocker-shaped parts of the pelvis.
Notice that you have large scope for movement. Notice also when you go so far forwards that you leave them and start to sit on your thigh bones. Conversely, notice when you go so far backwards that you leave them and start to sit on the base of your spine.

Your pelvic floor, at the base of your torso-cylinder, is made largely of muscle tissue. You do not have an anatomical waist; this is an invention of the fashion and clothing industry. Neither is your "waist" your middle. That is, you do not have joints which intend you to bend at the centre of your torso. If you want to bend down, use the joints in your legs and tilt your torso at your hip joints. Your spine links the base of your cylinder to the top of your cylinder, your skull.

Your Legs: Your legs come away from your torso at your hip joints which might well be lower down than you think they are. They are not on the level of the top of your big hip bones (the iliac crests) but where the crease is when you bend your knees forwards. Your legs can move easily thanks to your hip joints, knee joints, ankle joints and the joints in your toes. It is important to use these joints. Note that your knee joint is slightly below your knee cap. Your ankle joint is between the two knobbly bits at the bottom of your lower leg bone. Your heel extends behind that joint.

Your Arms and Hands: Your arms are longer than you perhaps think they are; they can be considered to include the collar bone.[3] It can be helpful to think of the first arm joint being the joint between collar bone and breast bone. You then have four arm joints: breast bone, shoulder, elbow, wrist. Look at your hands, at the palms and backs of them. Note that the creases at the base of your fingers on the palm side do not correspond to your knuckles on the back of your hand. Your finger joints are where your knuckles are, not where the creases are.

We will continue to return to basic anatomy and physiology when it is useful to do so. However, although we have looked at separate parts of the body, remember that you and your body are an integrated whole. What you do with your feet, for example, will have an impact on the balance of your head and vice versa. And all of that will have an impact on your total functioning.

Exploration 8: Exploring inter-connectedness
8.1 Sit on a firm-seated chair in a definite slump. Try raising an arm to about shoulder height and notice how much effort you need.

8.2 Now make sure your feet are firmly on the floor and that you are sitting on your sitting bones. Sit tall but not tense, with your eyes looking ahead but not staring. Try raising your arm again and notice how much effort you need.

Most people find it easier to raise their arm if they are sitting tall but not tense. The ease of movement of one body part depends on the organisation of the whole body.

Centered Standing: A Fundamental Skill
Centered standing means standing with your body in its natural alignment so that it can deliver weight efficiently and the muscles can regain their intended elasticity. This means that

you can stand tall and open to the world without effort. It promotes healthy body functioning by giving your internal organs space to work properly. And on top of that, standing tall helps you feel calmer and more self-confident; this will help you to keep your head and think on your feet in a difficult teaching situation.

When standing in a centered way it is important to stay with thinking rather than trying to do anything. This might involve saying "no" quite firmly to the temptation to put yourself into a position in order to achieve a pre-conceived idea of how you should be standing. This might sound rather nebulous, but there are good reasons why we want to put the emphasis on thinking rather than doing.

By saying "no" to any desire to do (for example, stand up straight, pull our shoulders back, and all the other commands usually associated with "good" posture) we are asking the big sheet muscles, which are the ones which carry out these commands, to stop working so hard. The big sheet muscles are not the ones which nature intends to keep us upright and they tire quickly if that is what they are asked to do. This is an example of compensation at work. Engaging the sheet muscles is an emergency measure to keep us upright because the smaller, deeper, postural muscles are not working properly. When told to stand or sit up straight, most of us who habitually stand or sit slightly slumped will react by engaging those sheet muscles and probably collapse back into a slump soon after, as it is too tiring to keep this up for long. We are in the slump-stretch cycle.

The postural muscles which should be keeping us easily upright lie deep underneath the superficial sheet muscles (see figures 2 and 3). It is these postural muscles which we can coax into action by thinking. In this way we can redistribute muscle tone: the postural muscles become more toned, while the superficial muscles can release when not needed.

Remember that mind and muscle are connected. Our thoughts have an impact on our muscles and vice versa. It is up to us to learn to use that connection to our advantage.

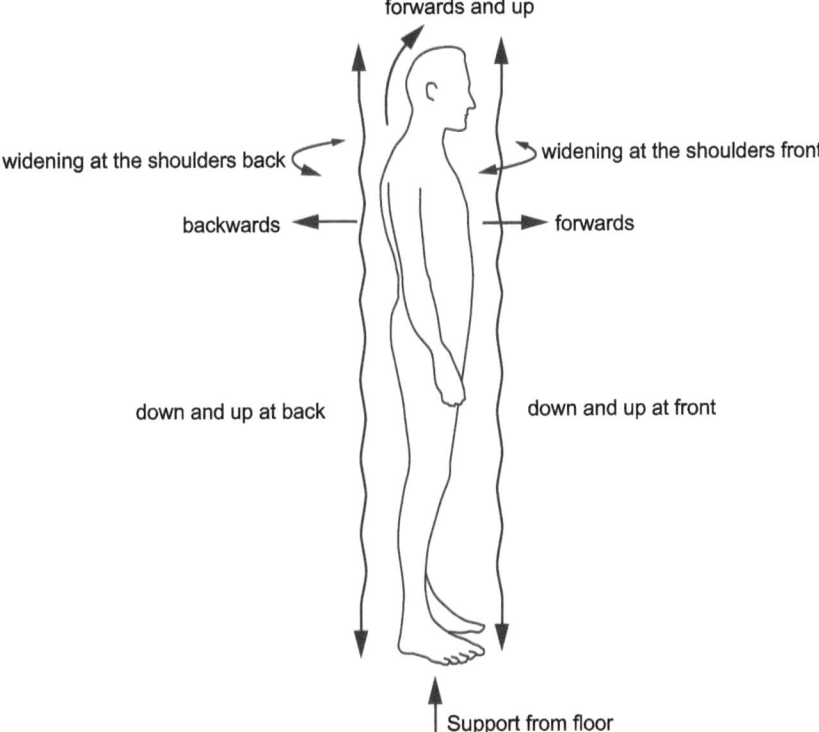

Figure 5: Centered standing

Exploration 9: Exploring centered standing

9.1 Practise the following five-step exploration of centered standing. Although you start off by thinking of individual body parts, with time and practice it becomes a total pattern and you can think of yourself as an integrated whole.

You might like to find a sensory stimulus (picture, sound, scent) which encapsulates for you the essence of centered standing and arrange things so that you encounter it every day. This will act as a reminder to you to center yourself and help it become a total pattern.

Step 1
Contact with Support: Stand on a firm surface with your feet about shoulder-width apart. Notice your contact with the ground: how it feels, its texture, temperature. Imagine the ground is coming up to meet the soles of your feet as your weight trickles down through your bones, into your feet, to meet the ground. Avoid locking your knees back. Think of your knees going forwards over your big toes and away from each other, but don't actually bend your knees.

Step 2
Lengthening Spine: At the same time as your feet are connecting with the ground, imagine that your head is swimming away from your heels and your heels are swimming away from your head. Imagine this lengthening in your back plane and in your front plane. Think: down and up in front and back.

Step 3
Balancing Head: Allow your neck muscles to let go of any unnecessary tension and your head to balance freely on the top of your spine. Make sure your head stays over your body and does not poke forwards, tortoise-fashion.

To help you, you can imagine a rod going from one ear to the other and the back of your head rotating around this horizontal axis. As the back of your head rolls slightly forwards and up, your nose will roll slightly down, but not so much that you are pushing down with your chin. Allow your eyes to look ahead at eye level, which might be a little higher than you are used to.

Step 4
Widening Shoulders: Think of widening across your shoulders at the front and back. Supported by your back, your arms are ready to be used. They are hanging freely and do not weigh down on your rib cage.

Step 5
Awareness of Internal and External Space: Find a 3-D you. Think of your front plane going forwards, your back plane going backwards. Think: forwards and backwards. Be aware of the external space behind you as well as in front.
Allow your eyes to soften and gently see what there is to see. Be aware of your peripheral vision, i.e. what you can see out of the corners of your eyes, while remaining focused in front.
Be aware of the sounds around you.
Allow your breath to flow, preferably breathing through your nose. Allow your face to relax. Allow your tongue gently to rest on the floor of your mouth, its tip behind your lower front teeth. Allow your jaw to relax and your lips lightly to touch each other.

Through delicately shifting your weight you can experience the combination of mobility and stability centered standing will give you. Keep your ankles free. Be aware of yourself as an integrated whole, from the soles of your feet to the crown of your head and beyond.

The ability to center yourself quickly and reliably even (or particularly) in stressful situations is essential to healthy living. Like all skills it needs to be learned and practised, and everyday life is full of opportunities: waiting at the supermarket check-out, at the bus stop, talking to colleagues. Use the practice opportunities daily life gives you. The more you practise, the easier centered standing will become and the more it will feel normal and natural. It will become the way you habitually stand.

Strength and Stability

When we feel we need special reserves of strength, particularly in difficult situations, we often tense up. We might do any or all of the following: retract the head, stiffen the neck, clench the jaw, brace the knees, make fists, fix the eyes, and almost certainly hold the breath as well. We are preparing for a fight – or to run away. The following exploration investigates the connection between physical tension, mental state, and strength and stability.

> **Exploration 10: Exploring strength and stability**
> For these explorations you will need a partner, maybe a good friend or family member.[4]
>
> **10.1** Stand with your feet parallel and about shoulder-width apart. Now turn yourself into a caricature of a Hulk: tense all your muscles, grimace, hold your breath, clench your fists, stare, brace your knees. Really enter into that state.
> Standing at right-angles to you, at the edge of your field of vision, your partner will now put the palm of one hand lightly on your breastbone and then on the corresponding part of your upper back. They are sensing your muscle tension. They can slowly put more pressure on you and see what happens. Do you topple over? Do you stay frozen and completely rigid?
>
> **10.2** Shake out all that tension and now stand centered. Remember to go through the five-step checklist: contact to support; lengthening spine; balancing head; widening shoulders; awareness of space.
> Your partner does the same test and notices the differences. Do you topple over as easily? Do you stand your ground but have

some mobility?
Be aware of which emotions are connected to each muscle state. Discuss this and any other aspects you and your partner notice.

10.3 Now think of a person or an activity which causes you mild anxiety. Allow your body to respond to those anxiety-inducing thoughts. You might well really feel your heart start pounding, your vision narrowing, your breathing become shallower. Your partner does the same test as before. What do you and your partner notice? How stable are you? How mobile?

10.4 Shake out that tension and now think of a person or an activity which gives you pleasure and makes you feel good. Your partner again does the test. What do you and your partner notice?

Probably you have noticed that a high degree of muscle tension does not in fact make you stronger. Most people notice that when they are tensing up either they become extremely unstable or they become rigid and locked. In addition, they tire quickly. In contrast, when they are standing in a centered way, they usually notice that they can combine stability with mobility and can often, quite effortlessly, withstand considerable pressure from their partner's hand. In fact, when things are going well and your core muscles are well toned, your partner can often lean against you with their whole body weight and you will not be pushed over nor feel you have to use effort to resist. In addition, you have probably noticed that the thought of something either pleasant or unpleasant is enough to trigger off a muscular response. This also means that we can help ourselves achieve centered standing (and gain more conscious control over our muscles) by gaining more control over our thoughts.

Exploring Everyday Activities

Let us now explore a few activities which teachers frequently perform: sitting; working at the computer; writing; holding a book. We will experiment with how we might apply what we have been looking at so far so that we can carry out these activities with greater ease.

The fundamental approach in line with the principles of this book is to focus on our habits of how we do what we do. However, it makes sense first to see what we can alter in our external conditions (for instance, furniture) to make things easier for ourselves, and then to see what we can alter in our response to those external conditions. In practice, in many teaching situations our control over our external environment may well be limited. Yet perhaps you are lucky and do have some control. If so, it might be worth taking a look at the chairs, for example. Do they slope backwards? If they do, perhaps you can get some that do not. When you read a book, you can use a book stand. When writing you can use a writing slope. Or even better, use a high standing desk and perch on a bar stool. Experiment with what helps you.

However, even with an ideal external set-up and the most ergonomic furniture, it is still more than likely that old unhelpful habits will come to the fore and we might well develop aches and pains. It is therefore essential that we learn how to deal with those external conditions, whatever shape or form they may take, in a way which does least damage to ourselves. As a first step, this means becoming aware of the habits which accompany us through our everyday lives. What habits do you have surrounding sitting at the computer, holding a pen, reading a book? And as a second step, it means learning to recognise that some of those habits might be contributing to our woes and that we can learn different, more helpful habits, which keep us in tune with our natural functioning and minimise compensation.

Sitting

First, get the externals to work for you. What kind of chair do you sit on? Most chairs in institutions are not bought with thought for the people who will have to use them, but for reasons of cost and space, that is, they have to be cheap and stackable. They are often made of plastic, have moulded seats, hard edges, and slope backwards. Assuming that you have to use what you are given, then at least do not ruin your health. If your chairs do slope backwards, then you might like to invest in a firm seating wedge. Look online for offers, but make sure it is firm enough. Or raise the back legs of the chair by putting something underneath them. This will make it easier not to slump. If you have long legs you might find it easier to put something on the chair seat to raise you up; conversely if you have short legs, you might find it easier to put something under your feet, a low stool or even telephone books, for example. Your feet should be able to rest fully on the floor and your knees should be slightly lower than your hip joints. You might find it helpful to sit further forwards on the chair. And you can of course move and change position. Sitting is a dynamic activity.

Although probably impracticable if you work at an institution, at home you might like to experiment with perching. The ubiquitousness of chairs is actually a relatively modern phenomenon, and there are still many parts of the world where to squat or sit cross-legged on the floor is the norm.[5] But even in Europe, particularly when writing or reading, it was until relatively recently not unusual to perch on tall stools (similar to modern bar stools). Clerks in the Victorian era regularly perched at their standing desks while writing in their ledgers. Perching has the benefits of more mobility, and it is easier to remain grounded, to keep your spine lengthening, your legs coming away from your torso at more than 90°, and your arms extending away from your torso. However, most of us have to use what we are given, at least at the workplace. The following exploration is intended to help you sit in a more centered way, whatever you are sitting on.

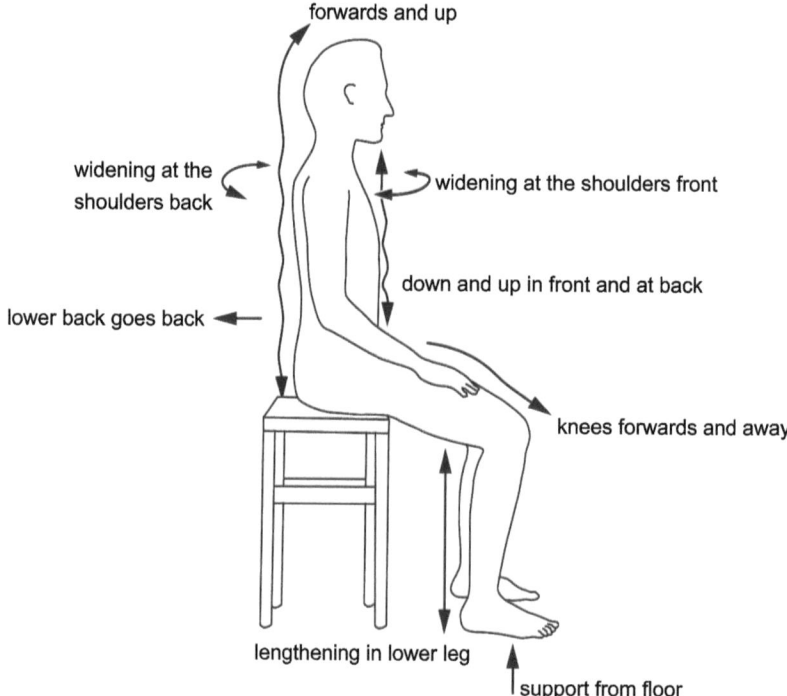

Figure 6: Centered sitting

Exploration 11: Exploring centered sitting

11.1 Before you start make sure both your feet are fully on the ground. Imagine the ground is rising to meet your feet and your feet are going down to meet the ground.

Step 1

Make sure you're sitting on your sitting bones, not your tailbone or thigh bones. Make sure you are not tightening your thighs and pulling your legs into your torso. Instead, you can imagine your knees are going forwards and a little away from each other, and that you have long thighs.

Step 2

Be very sure that you are not pulling in your lower back; think of your back going back and be aware of the space behind you.

Step 3

Now allow your head and tailbone to swim away from each other. Think also of your length in front. And allow your shoulders to widen across the front and back.

Step 4

Be aware of your movement possibilities. Sitting is dynamic. On your sitting bones rock gently forwards thinking of your forehead leading, keeping your spine long and head integrated (i.e. not retracted at any moment of the tilt forwards). Make sure your knees do not go together as you tilt forwards. Then rock backwards. Notice how much movement is possible while still remaining centered and balanced on your sitting bones.

11.2 Become aware of your sitting habits. Do you habitually cross your legs, sit on the base of your spine, wrap your legs around the chair legs, lift your heels off the floor, tighten your thighs, pull your head back and down, clench your jaw, hold your breath? If you notice yourself doing any of these, stop and reorganise yourself.

Working at the Computer

Most of us spend time in front of a computer screen so it is worthwhile learning how to do so with the least damage to ourselves.

Exploration 12: Exploring using a computer
12.1 Make sure you are sitting in a centered way (exploration 11). If you need to come forwards towards the screen, make sure you do so by rocking on your sitting bones and keeping a long spine. Think of allowing your head to lead your torso up and then forwards. Do not come forwards by poking your head forwards or bending at your "waist".

Step 1
As you did in the active resting exploration (exploration 5), think of your long, wing-like arms, which are connected to your breastbone. Leading with the tips of your fingers, allow your arms to move forwards so that your fingers lightly come to rest on the keyboard. Keep the idea of long fingers and a strong supporting torso going as you type.

Remember that you need very little muscle effort to operate a computer. The main strength you need is to support your arms to prevent them weighing down on your rib cage and impairing your breathing. This support comes from your well-functioning spine and the postural muscles attached to it, not your upper arms, shoulders, or neck. This is important. Be careful not to let your shoulders hunch forwards or up towards your ears.

Step 2
Think of having balloons lodged between your upper arms and the side of your body to keep your arms buoyant. Make sure that you are not letting your lower back come forwards as your arms come forwards. Think "back stays back". Remember your depth as well as length and width.

Step 3
Be aware of the space all around you, even when focusing on the screen in front. Do not allow yourself to get pulled down or sucked forwards into the screen. Think of the space between it and you; you might like to think of magnetic repulsion between the screen and you. Think of the space behind you.

Take frequent breaks. Rest your eyes by changing their focus. Get up and stretch your legs.

Writing by hand

Despite prevalent computer use, many teachers often find themselves writing by hand, for example when marking papers. If you do a lot of writing by hand, it would be worth getting hold of a writing slope. This will help you stay taller and more upright while writing and encourages a freer use of the hand. Our forefathers obviously knew their benefits as some illustrations of scribes and monks show them perching and writing at sloping lecterns. If you can organise such a set-up, that is ideal. If feasible, you might also like to change your writing implement to pencil or fountain pen as these allow more flexibility in angle and pressure than ballpoint pens.

Exploration 13: Exploring writing by hand
13.1 Make sure you are sitting in a centered way (exploration 11). Sit as close to the desk as possible, without pressing against it. Remember also to think of your long, wing-like arms, coming out away from your back and moving from the finger-tips (exploration 12).

Step 1
Bring your non-writing hand, elbow and forearm to rest on the desk or writing slope. Allow your elbow and forearm to take your

weight. Be careful to maintain your centered sitting as you do so. Do not collapse onto your non-writing arm.

Step 2
Allow your long fingers to take on the shape of your writing implement. Avoid grasping it; you need very little strength to hold a pen or pencil. Keep your wrist free.
When you rotate your lower arm to take hold of your writing implement, note that it is the thumb-side which rotates around the little finger side.

Step 3
Bring your writing hand up to rest on the desk or writing slope. Keep your hand free. Imagine your fingers to be long and coming away from your wrists. Allow your wrists and elbows to swim away from each other.

On a piece of rough paper you can experiment with making big, flowing writing shapes while keeping your wrist free, fingers lengthening away from your wrist, and your neck and shoulders uninvolved.
How much pressure on the paper do you really need? Can you write with less than you usually do? This might well also depend on your writing implement. Monitor your jaw and tongue. Are they released and at rest? Is your breathing free?

Reading
A sloping book holder, like a writing slope, will help you to stay tall and more upright, and save you holding the book. It is worth getting a solidly made one, which can be used for books of various sizes and weights. If you use an e-reader, then put that on the slope. If you do not have a slope to hand then you can try to improvise one. In some trains and while flying, for example, you can put the tray table down and lean the book

against the back of the seat in front.

Exploration 14: Exploring reading
14.1 If you are reading sitting down, then remember to sit in a centered way (exploration 11).

Step 1
If possible, hold or put the book (e-reader) at eye level. If you need to look down, let your head rotate around the imaginary horizontal rod through your ears (exploration 9). Allow your eyes to initiate the movement; this will help to release your neck muscles. Stay tall. It is important not to look down by collapsing at the breast bone and slumping or by poking your head forwards. Explore also how much independence your eyes have from your head position.

Step 2
Remember to keep the thought of your back going back especially when you stretch your arms forwards to turn the pages; think of keeping your distance from what you are reading.

Step 3
If you are holding the book, do not do so by tensing your upper arms, neck and shoulders. Use your back instead; think again of your big wing-like arms which come out of your back.

Monitor your tongue and jaw and allow them to release and rest. Allow your eyes to read gently; rest them if necessary by changing focus or closing them. Keep your breath flowing.

If you are able to integrate even only some of these explorations into your everyday life, you will notice that you can get through a day with less wear and tear. And getting through the day with less wear and tear will mean you feel better in every way. You will probably notice that you are calmer, more alert, and have more energy.

---

[1] See Barbara Conable, *How to learn the Alexander Technique. A Manual for Students* (Andover Press, Portland OR, 1995)
[2] See Robert Beverly Hale and Terence Coyle, *Albinus on Anatomy* (Dover Publications, New York, 1988)
[3] See Conable, op. cit., pp.52-3
[4] Thanks to Alan Mars for this exploration.
[5] See Galen Cranz, *The Chair: Rethinking Culture, Body, and Design* (W.W.Norton, New York, 1998), pp.176ff

3

YOUR VOCAL WELL-BEING

Where there is no instrument there can be no body; where there is no body there can be no sound. (Leonardo Da Vinci)

As a teacher, your voice is your most important teaching tool; without it you are lost. Yet vocal problems are one of the most common reasons for sickness amongst teachers. Perhaps this is not surprising as learning the psycho-physical skills of healthy voice use is not generally part of teacher training. One can speculate as to the reasons for this. It might be a consequence of a once widespread notion that education is about knowledge; it is the teacher's job to impart knowledge and the pupil's to soak it up. In its more positive form this notion manifests itself in the assumption that good teachers focus on developing new teaching methods and materials, rather than on looking after themselves. The lack of training in healthy voice use might also be due to an underestimation in society as a whole of the importance of the voice in communication and human interaction. And perhaps it might also be a consequence of the widespread idea that your voice is a matter of luck. Either you have a good, healthy voice or you do not and there is nothing you can do about it.

Of course, that is not true. How you use and look after your voice is crucial to how healthy it is and remains. And you can learn to use your voice with less strain and more impact. Giving teachers some basic vocal training creates a potential win-win situation. Not only does the vocally aware teacher benefit in terms of personal well-being and improved communication skills, but the education institution benefits in terms of reduced sickness and related costs, and the students in terms of improved teaching and easier learning.

The human voice is a huge subject. And it is one where opinions can divide remarkably quickly; disagreements and contradictions between vocal coaches abound. What follows here can only be an overview of the most important points. To give each aspect detailed treatment would fill several books and would probably not really be what most teachers would find most useful. This chapter will focus on healthy breathing and voicing. As this and the previous chapter give you the foundations for healthy speaking, it is best to familiarise yourself with their contents first before moving on to chapters five and seven which focus on speaking and performing skills. In order to get an overview of how each element of voice work builds on another, have a look at the voice pyramid in figure 7.

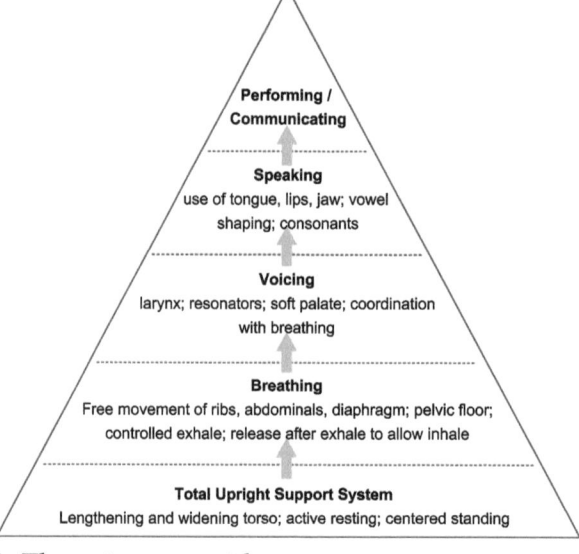

Figure 7: The voice pyramid

Your Body is your Instrument

You are a musical instrument. The condition of your body matters and makes a difference to the kind of sound you make and the ease with which you make it. Think of an acoustic guitar. If it is misshapen and out of tune, it will be hard to play and almost impossible to make a pleasant sound which invites people to listen. When it is well aligned and well tuned, with neither too much nor too little tension in the strings, it will be much easier to play and the sounds it makes will be pleasant. It will also be much more responsive to the player's musical intention. Similarly, when your body, your musical instrument, is well aligned, with neither too much nor too little tension, then you, the musician, can speak with ease, your voice is much more likely to invite others to listen, and it is much more likely to be responsive to your communicative intention.

Exploration 15: Exploring your body-voice connection

15.1 You can do this exploration either on your own or in a group.

Step 1

In sitting, go into your "best" slump. Exaggerate.
Let your head roll back and down so shortening your neck and compressing your spine. Lose good contact with the floor by, for example, raising your heels off the floor. Roll back off your sitting bones so that you are sitting on the base of your spine. Allow your shoulders to round so your breastbone collapses. Stare at the floor. In short, do everything you know you shouldn't.
Then sing the vowel "ah" (as in "far") on any one pitch. How do you feel? Then repeat. How does your voice sound? If you're doing this with others (each person can choose their own pitch), repeat again. How does the group sound?

What adjectives would you use to describe your sound and

feeling? Tired? Dull? Colourless? Depressed? Effortful? If you are in a group, how harmonious was the group sound?

Step 2
Then, still seated, center yourself.
Make sure you have both feet on the ground and that you are sitting on your sitting bones. Allow your back to keep lengthening and widening and your head to balance on the top of your spine. Keep your eyes looking ahead and be aware of your peripheral vision. Send your awareness out to the space behind you, then cultivate 360° awareness.
Vocalise again. How do you feel? How do you sound?

What differences do you notice to the first time round? More energy? Brighter sound? Held for longer? Felt easier? If you are in a group, was the group sound more harmonious?

As you have probably just now experienced in this exploration, centering is an essential skill as regards ease of vocalisation and making the most of your voice. Your body needs to be lengthening and widening for your vocal apparatus to work efficiently. You will experience this as greater ease and vocal longevity. If necessary, have another look at the previous chapter to revise centering.

As in the previous chapter, you should do all the explorations with centering in mind. And also as in the previous chapter, it is essential to keep your field of awareness wide and unified. Keep your eyes open and looking at eye level. In your awareness, engage with the space around you, including above, below, and behind you. Even though you may feel the need to "concentrate", you should not do this by closing your eyes, drifting off into your interior world, or narrowing your field of vision, as these will in turn lead to a narrowing of your body and your mind. For more on this important aspect please see the "Note on Concentration" in chapter eight.

How to Use your Instrument: The Basics
Your Spine
As you saw in the previous chapter, your spine is your central support. If it is out of alignment (which is not the same thing as not being perfectly straight), then not only does moving become more difficult than it need be, speaking does also. The deep postural muscles will not be able to work properly and other muscles will compensate. If the lumbar area is not supporting, abdominal muscles must take over the job and therefore are not free to be used for breathing. Similarly, if the thoracic spine is not doing its job of supporting the ribcage and shoulder girdle, the rib muscles have to take over and so are not available for rib mobility which is essential for easy breathing. If the vertebrae of the neck are not aligned and the head is not balancing freely, then the neck and throat muscles tighten, which means the channel for the voice is constricted. And with a tight neck, it is very hard for the jaw muscles, larynx, and tongue root to release, all of which again obstructs easy vocal use.

Your Trampolines
Before we look at how your body produces voiced sound we need to take a look at some important places of elasticity in your body. These are your trampolines. These are important as they need to be toned in order for breathing and vocalisation to work easily. We want them to be neither sluggish nor over-tensed, but toned and elastic.

The three most important trampolines which need to be working and coordinating well in vocalisation are your pelvic floor, your diaphragm, and your soft palate. These three areas are linked via the nervous system and any stiffening in one will lead to stiffening in the others.[1]

Your pelvic floor: This is an elastic cat's cradle of muscles, slung at the base of your torso. It is quite literally the muscular floor of your torso. In order to keep your breath flowing and support your voice it is important that your pelvic floor is kept toned and elastic.

> **Exploration 16: Exploring your pelvic floor**
> **16.1** Lie in the active resting position (see exploration 5). Then gradually activate your pelvic floor by contracting the muscles. You can think of pulling your genitalia up inside you. At the same time breathe out slowly. Make sure you are not tensing any other body parts unnecessarily (buttocks, jaw, face). Keep breathing. Think of a diagonal connection between your pelvic floor and the middle of your lower back. Allow your lower back to go down into the floor as you activate your pelvic floor and exhale. Allow a full release after exhalation.

For many people conscious activation is necessary, at least at the beginning, in order to awaken their mind-muscle connection to their pelvic floor. But once activated, centered standing and well-functioning postural muscles will help keep the pelvic floor toned.

Your diaphragm: The diaphragm is a large membrane which separates your lungs from your intestines and alters the volumes of the thoracic cavity and abdominal cavity. It is the largest single muscle in your body. When at rest, it is domed like an umbrella. When it contracts, it drops down and flattens, increasing the volume of the thoracic cavity. Air rushes in. You inhale. When the diaphragm returns to rest it releases upwards, the volume of the thoracic cavity decreases and air escapes. You exhale. (For more on breathing and the movement of the ribs see the relevant section later in this chapter.) It is worth noting that the diaphragm is, then, primarily a muscle of inhalation, not exhalation. This might well not be what you (and others) believe.

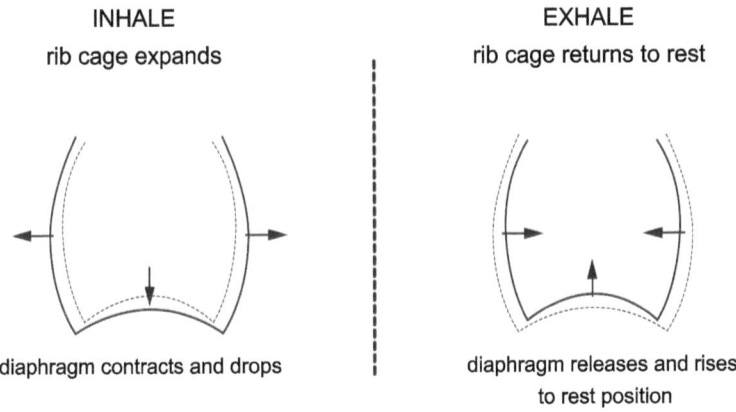

Figure 8: Movement of the diaphragm and ribcage

It can be helpful to think of both the upward and downward movement of the diaphragm as easy, free softening. Just like the rest of you, your diaphragm needs to be able to move freely in order to function efficiently. We cannot directly control the movement of the diaphragm and we cannot directly feel what it is doing. But we can connect with it by picturing its movement. And of course, its movement will be indirectly affected by other muscles and parts of the body. In this connection it is above all worth knowing that freedom in your knees is important as they connect (via muscles) to your diaphragm. If your knees are locked back, your diaphragm cannot move freely and the mobility of your lower back is also compromised. You do not need actually to bend your knees forwards, but do make sure you are not jamming them backwards. The thought of sending your knees forwards and away from each other, which you encountered in centered standing and sitting, is again helpful here.

Exploration 17: Exploring your diaphragm

17.1 Lie in the active resting position.

As you gently let however much air you have go on a gentle, sustained hiss, picture your diaphragm softening and rising towards your collarbone. Do not prepare to breathe out with any special inhale or other preparation. Do not push the air out; think of softening the diaphragm to allow the air to flow out.

Then picture your diaphragm dropping down towards your pelvic floor. After a pause the air will rush back in. If possible, close your mouth and let it in through your nose. Repeat a few times to establish a breathing cycle.

As the air leaves your lungs, your abdominal wall should move down towards your back. It is being pulled from the inside as the diaphragm releases upwards. Do not add any extra pull or push. This is reactive movement, not effort by the external abdominal muscles.[2] As the inner abdominal muscles release, the abdominal wall should move away from your back and the air rushes in. (For more on this, see the section on breathing in this chapter.)

Your soft palate: Run your tongue or a clean finger back along the roof of your mouth, from your upper front teeth as far back as you can without gagging. You will notice that the front of the roof of your mouth is hard and bony, it domes upwards in the middle, and that if you go far enough back, it becomes soft. The front bit is your alveolar ridge, the domed bit is your hard palate and the soft bit at the back is your soft palate. The alveolar ridge and hard palate are bone, the soft palate is muscle.

In order to have a healthy, resonant voice and to speak expressively, it is essential to have a toned and responsive soft palate. Many of us have either sluggish, collapsed soft palates or stiff, unduly tensed ones. If it is collapsed your voice will be dull, overly nasal and the sound muffled, often leading to problems with audibility. The common, mistaken, response to this is to push and strain, leading to a sore throat, hoarseness, or even voice loss. If the soft palate is stiff and unresponsive, a thin, monotonous voice is often the result. Thus, if the soft palate is not working properly, we compromise both our vocal health and our ability to communicate easily and effectively.

To start off with, it is essential to learn to raise and lower your soft palate. This is important as lifting it increases the space inside your mouth (oral cavity) and will therefore help to increase the volume and resonance of your voice without any strain. By minimising nasality, a raised soft palate also gives your voice a brighter colour and helps it to carry better. When the muscles have become toned and alive, they can respond involuntarily to intention and emotion, that is, the soft palate will move without you having to do it consciously. This is what we need for expressive speaking with a healthy voice.

Exploration 18: Exploring your soft palate
18.1 Center yourself. Look into your wide-open mouth with a mirror. Use a torch if necessary. Locate your soft palate. The

fleshy appendage hanging down at the back of your mouth is the uvula.

Still looking inside your mouth and with your tongue resting (but not pushing down) on the floor of your mouth, say "ah" and notice what happens to your palate. Now yawn heartily (just breath, no voice at all). Notice what happens. Now sing a high note on an "ah" vowel sound. Notice what happens.

Ideally, you should be seeing upward movement in the soft palate in all three cases. If not, persevere and consciously try to raise the palate. Stay centered. Notice that your palate lifts itself into a domed shape.

18.2 Raise your soft palate and say or sing an "ah" on one pitch. Now gently pinch your nostrils and keep vocalising. If your soft palate is domed, you should not hear any difference in sound. If it is not domed enough, you will hear, when you pinch your nostrils, that your voice becomes nasal; you sound like you have a heavy cold. Persevere until you do not hear any difference in sound. (This works because a raised soft palate seals off the entrance to the nasal cavity; all the air is directed through your mouth instead.)

18.3 Roll your head and hum. Allow your tongue to rest on the floor of your mouth. Be aware of the space between the back of your tongue and your soft palate. The space between them will change as you roll your head, but they should never touch. It will narrow when you have your head dropped forwards and increase when your head is dropped back. Be careful not to push your tongue down onto the floor of your mouth. If palate and tongue do touch when your head is forwards, raise your palate, don't push down on your tongue, in order to create space.[3]

18.4 This exploration might be called "The rose and the rainbow". Center yourself. Imagine you are holding a beautifully scented rose in one hand. Bring that hand to your nose. Inhale through your nose and dome your soft palate while keeping your lips lightly together as if you were inhaling the beautiful scent and want to enjoy it to the full. Then make a sound of appreciation, "mmmm", and imagine sending it up and over a rainbow into the space around you.

You might notice that your eyes widen and brighten, your nostrils dilate, and that your face lifts and widens at the cheekbones when you imagine inhaling a beautiful scent. Welcome this and allow it to happen. However, do not try to raise the soft palate by making Bambi eyes, grinning, or dilating the nostrils.

When your soft palate is toned and elastic, your face and eyes will become more expressive, open, and responsive. You might experience widening of the face at the cheek bones. You get a natural face lift.

Breathing in through the nose helps the soft palate to dome. Your palate should be active on the in and the out breath, not fixed in position. It is elastic, moving in accordance with your breath flow. However, during all this, it is important that your larynx stays released down and your throat stays open.

More Basics: How to Produce Voiced Sound

Think again of an acoustic guitar. In order for there to be sound there needs to be a finger or plectrum plucking a string which vibrates. These vibrations are amplified by the guitar body so that we can hear them. That is, in order for there to be audible sound, three elements (excitor, vibrator, resonator) are needed. Firstly, there is an excitor (the finger or plectrum) which causes a vibrator (the string) to vibrate. The sound waves created by the vibrations are then amplified in the resonator (the guitar body) so that they can become resonant sound.

Voice production in humans happens in a similar manner.

Put very simply, the outbreath (the excitor) causes the vocal folds (the vibrator) in the larynx to vibrate when the folds are brought together. This in turn creates sound waves which are amplified in the resonators, primarily of the throat and mouth, to make a rich, audible sound. Note that we make sound on the outbreath, not when we breathe in.

In all the explorations involving vocalisation it is important to focus on function rather than sound. It is very tempting to listen to the sounds we make, rather than paying attention to how we make those sounds. It is, however, important that we do not allow ourselves to focus on sound. We need to focus on the function of making sound, rather than the sound itself, in the knowledge that if the body is working as it is intended to, the sound will look after itself. This is important as otherwise we can undo any re-training in how we use ourselves in our attempts to meet our preconceived ideas of how we should sound. We need to allow sound to be a by-product of function. If we are using ourselves well, then all will be well.

Your Breath: The Excitor
Without breath there can be no voice. But even more than that: without breath we cannot live. Every time air flows into our lungs we are given oxygen with which we nourish every cell in our body. And every time air leaves our lungs we rid ourselves of the waste products of used up oxygen. Breathing thus takes place not only in the lungs but at a deep molecular level throughout the body. Because respiration is such a fundamental life function we are programmed to breathe rhythmically and automatically from our first minutes after birth onwards for the rest of our lives. It is important to realise this. It means that we do not actively have to take in air; air will flow into our lungs

of its own accord, if we allow it to and do not interfere with that cyclical process which is breathing.

There is, however, a multiplicity of ways of interfering with this process, so the great challenge is to stop doing the interfering and let the process work on its own. But how does the process work? Very simply, when the space in the chest cavity increases, air flows in through the nose or mouth to fill the space. Conversely, when we decrease the size of the chest cavity, air flows out. The space in the chest cavity is made larger by the rib cage expanding as the ribs rotate up and out to the sides (like bucket handles). At the same time, as you have already read, the diaphragm contracts down. It is made smaller by the ribs slowly returning to their rest position and the diaphragm releasing upwards (look again at figure 8). And as you noticed when exploring your diaphragm (in exploration 17), there is also reactive movement in your abdominals. Ideally, you should notice your breastbone move, but be aware that you do not breathe by raising and lowering your shoulders.

It is important to understand that we need mobility in the ribs in order to breathe efficiently. Unfortunately, in English we talk of the "rib cage" which is a highly misleading term, suggesting as it does fixity and imprisonment. In fact, the function of the ribs is protection of the lungs and movement, not imprisonment and fixing. It is worth bearing this in mind.

For easy and efficient breathing it is necessary to have freedom in the ribs, diaphragm and inner abdominals. And in order for that to happen, the total body support system, which you looked at in the previous chapter, needs to be working well. Interference may come from too much tension somewhere in the instrument: stiffening in the abdominals, immobile ribs, tightening in the throat, but also for example in the legs, knees, buttocks, lower back, neck. However, it is important to realise that it may also come from too little tension somewhere in the instrument, for example, sluggish breathing or postural muscles, which, as they are not working properly, cause other muscles to take over and compensate. Therefore we do need to have properly toned muscles in order to be able to "let go" of the unnecessary tension, otherwise compensation will occur.

The following explorations will help you become more aware of breath flow in your everyday life.

> **Exploration 19: Exploring your breath flow**
> **19.1** Very many of us have the habit of holding our breath and momentarily interrupting the flow of air.
> Notice when in your daily life you hold your breath. For example, when you unscrew a tight lid, thread a needle, pick something up from the floor, sit down, lift something heavy ...
> See if you can do the activity without holding your breath. Consciously focus on the exhale. Does performing the activity become easier?
>
> **19.2** Lie on the floor on your front and put your head to one side. Lightly put your hands on your lower ribs at your back, your finger tips pointing towards your spine. Without any special preparation or inhale, slowly exhale on a gentle hiss, using whatever air you happen to have.
>
> Remember to think of your spine lengthening as you do so. It is helpful not to think of sighing and letting the air go all at once, as this idea is often connected with collapse and shortening, but of allowing the air to escape slowly until it is all gone. Then close your mouth and notice how, if you do not interfere, after a small

pause the air will come in of its own accord through your nose.

Allow the small pause to happen, that is, wait. Do this several times; get a cycle going.

Notice also what is happening to your ribs. If they are free, you should notice that on the exhale your hands move down and towards each other and on the inhale up and away from each other. You might like to imagine you are breathing with your back. You might well feel that your back is opening on the inhale. Allow the whole of your back to be part of the movement which is breathing.

19.3 When you are feeling clear movement in your ribs, do the same exploration in the active resting position. Remember to start the cycle with an unprepared hiss. Do not take a special breath before you start hissing.
Go through several breathing cycles. Again, avoid the idea of sighing and letting all the air go quickly. Instead, allow the air to escape slowly. Keep allowing your spine to lengthen. Refuse to shorten. This is important.

Be aware of the movement in your abdomen, as well as in your ribs. Your abdomen should gently move down towards your spine on the exhale while the size of your ribcage diminishes, with most movement at the sides.

Then notice how at the end of each exhale the ribs and abdomen want to spring back and reverse the process. Allow this release to happen. This is important. Let the air come in through your nose. Focus on softening and releasing, then the ribs and abdominals are more likely to move freely; do not try to manufacture movement.

19.4 When that is going well, try the same exploration in centered

standing. Notice the movement in your ribs and abdomen. Once again, be very careful not to shorten on the exhale.
Allow your shoulders to be quiet and largely uninvolved in the whole process.

Why hiss? Gentle hissing is often useful as, unlike whispering, it does not involve the larynx. When we hiss, the air flow is disturbed by the obstruction formed by the tongue touching the roof of the mouth, just behind the upper front teeth. When we whisper, we need to bring the laryngeal vocal folds slightly together in order to disturb the air flow. Hissing is therefore less likely to trigger off habits of excess laryngeal tension and is safer, particularly if you have or have had nodules on your vocal folds.[4]

Why promote breathing in through the nose? Inhaling through the nose has several advantages: it adjusts the air temperature to body temperature before the air enters deeper into the body; it filters and disinfects the air; it moistens the air if it is too dry; it helps the soft palate to be elastic and responsive; it protects the vocal folds from dehydration and infection; and it slows down the breathing process giving us more time to release and say "no" to any unnecessary habitual tightening. When speaking or singing we might sometimes need to take in air faster; then we can use nose and mouth breathing. But otherwise, when we do not need air fast, for example when we are sitting at a desk, walking down the street, watching TV, we can breathe in and out through the nose. To facilitate this (amongst other benefits), you might like to massage your face with your finger tips, working away from your nostrils along your cheekbones to the sides of your face.

Your Vocal Well-Being

Your Larynx: The Vibrator

This is a structure of cartilage suspended in your throat by a complex system of small muscles. It is also indirectly connected to your tongue, which means that unnecessary tongue root tension will disturb the suspension of the larynx. In order for your larynx to work well it needs to be freely suspended, and for this the muscles of your neck and torso need to be in balance, neither doing too much nor too little. This is crucial and another reason, in addition to those already mentioned, why it is important for your head to balance on the top of your spine and for your torso to be lengthening and widening.

Inside the larynx, running from front to back, there are two vocal folds, whose edges meet and go apart again very fast ("vibrate") when air coming up from the lungs passes through the gap between them. This vibration causes the air to oscillate at a certain frequency and is the source of sound. We can alter the size of the space between the edges of the folds, their density and length. This determines pitch and influences our voice quality, including how breathy our voice is. These fine adjustments happen largely without our conscious control.

Exploration 20: Exploring your larynx

20.1 Locate your larynx. Place a finger or two gently on the front of your throat and feel for a lump. This is the thyroid cartilage, the main housing of your larynx. It is often more pronounced in men than in women and called the Adam's apple.

20.2 For this exploration of laryngeal suspension it is useful to become a four-footed animal. The point of this is to allow the larynx to hang so it can find its own resting place without being pulled by uncoordinated neck muscles. By going onto all fours we are using gravity to help us.

Step 1
Go down on your hands and knees. You might like to kneel on a rug or carpet. Make sure the heels of your hands are under your shoulders, and your knee caps under your hip joints. Your fingers point forwards, your palms are open. Let as much of your palms and the tops of your feet make contact with the floor as possible.

Step 2
Think of your head swimming away from your tailbone and vice versa, keeping your spine long and being careful not to lift your face up to look forwards; you should be looking at the floor. Remember you are a four-footed animal and have eyes at the front of your head.

Step 3
Think of your weight trickling down through your thighs and knees, arms and hands into the floor. At the same time you are thinking of your hip joints moving away from your knees, and your shoulders moving away from your wrists.

Step 4
Imagine that your front plane (your face, jaw, tongue, throat, larynx, chest, belly) is falling down towards the floor. Let it all hang. While that is all hanging, imagine that your back plane (your back, the back of your neck, the back of your head, the backs of your calves) rises towards the ceiling. We are after a nice antagonistic stretch between down and up. Remember: stay with the thinking. We are connecting mind with muscle.

Step 5
When that is going well, play around with shifting more weight onto your hands, then more onto your knees, while keeping that antagonistic stretch going and your spine long and integrated.

Remember to let your larynx hang.

Step 6
Then gently vocalise: hum, sing "ah" on one pitch. Let the sound drop down into the floor through your face.

A very useful exploration is "the whispered ah". This can be used for breathing re-education and re-education of habits around vocalisation. As regards breathing re-education, our use of hissing in exploration 19 covers the same ground of allowing reflexive breathing to happen. In this exploration we will use "the whispered ah" to encourage laryngeal release.[5]

Exploration 21: Exploring releasing the larynx with "the whispered ah"

21.1 As always, make sure you are standing in a centered way.

Step 1
Allow your tongue to rest lightly on the floor of your mouth, but don't push it down. You can monitor this by putting the ball of your thumb on the soft fleshy part under your chin, in the horseshoe formed by your jaw bone. You should not feel any pressure being exerted on your thumb.

Step 2
While keeping your lips lightly together, let your jaw drop, your soft palate rise and your face lift and widen at the cheekbones. You might like to imagine an inner smile, a smile not with your lips, but with your eyes. It often helps to think of something funny or a bit naughty. You are breathing normally in and out through your nose.

Step 3
At the same time, allow your larynx to drop. You might well really feel it move down, but don't push or chase that sensation. Think again of an antagonistic stretch, this time between your larynx and your soft palate: down – up.

Step 4
On an unprepared exhale, with whatever air you have, simply allow your jaw to drop more to open your mouth and allow the air to flow out slowly without allowing your soft palate to collapse, your larynx to rise, or your tongue to push down or bunch up at the back. Keep the antagonistic stretch on the exhale and make a whispered "ah" sound. Note that this is not a sigh, with all the air escaping in a rush and often accompanied by collapse, but a naturally controlled exhale.

Step 5
When you have no air left, close your mouth, allow release of the ribs and abdomen, wait and let the air in through your nose.

Repeat several times; get a cycle going. Monitor any tension in your throat, tongue, jaw. The sound should be a clear vowel, whispered but without any throatiness.

21.2 You might find it easier to do "the whispered ah" using the "ng" sound to get into the "ah". This also facilitates breathing through the nose and awareness of the soft palate and tongue.[6]

Step 1
In centered standing let your jaw drop so your mouth is open. Now anchor the tip of your tongue behind your lower front teeth and place the back of your tongue on the ridge between soft and hard palate, the position for the "ng" sound (as in "running", "doing", etc). This will make you breathe through your nose as you have blocked off the oral passage. Continue to breathe normally.

Step 2
Allow your larynx to drop and soft palate to rise; the back of your tongue continues to touch the roof of your mouth.

Step 3
On an unprepared exhale allow the back of your tongue to lose contact with the roof of your mouth, while keeping the tip anchored behind the lower front teeth. You will be making an "ah" sound. Let it make contact again for the inhale. Repeat several times, making fine movements with the tongue. Do not push your tongue down, it only needs to lose contact minimally with the roof of your mouth. Monitor any tongue root tension with the ball of your thumb under your jaw. You should not feel any.

Why is whispering beneficial? Well, it helps us engage the vocal folds in a way which is not associated with our usual, often harmful, vocal habits. By whispering we can learn to vocalise without our usual habits of poor use.[7] The "whispered ah" also has a very calming yet energising effect and is very useful in moments of stress.

Your Oral Cavity, Nasal Passage, and more: The Resonators
Sound waves are amplified as they meet surfaces of different textures and shapes. The harder the surface, the greater the amplification as the sound waves bounce off the hard surfaces. The result is a louder sound. In the human body, these hard surfaces can be bone, cartilage or toned muscle. Soft, flabby tissue will have the opposite effect of absorbing sound. In practice the most important and effective resonators are hard-surfaced cavities of the body such as the mouth, nose, sinus hollows, chest and skull.

Exploring a highly skilled use of the resonators is beyond

the scope of this book; it is the province above all of singers and actors. However, it is useful for those in speaking professions to learn to use the mid to upper resonators in the nose-eyes area, as this is a key to audibility, clarity, and an energised voice. If we do not use the facial resonators then our voice sounds as if it is trapped in our throat – which it, more or less, is. This often feels laboured to the speaker and is effortful to listen to.

This nose-eyes area is sometimes called "the mask". This is, perhaps, an unfortunate term as it suggests rigidity and concealment, whereas what we want is the exact opposite: allowing the face to be mobile and open, and the voice to blossom and be heard. Using the resonators in the nose-eyes area in particular is not to be confused with nasality, which is a product of the exclusive use of the nasal resonators to make a one-dimensional sound. This happens when the voice largely escapes from the nose instead of the mouth, because the mouth is blocked by a sluggish soft palate or a bunched up tongue.

As so often when talking about the body and the voice in particular, we need to clarify our terms. Using the resonators is not to be confused with "projection" which suggests "throwing" your voice out to your audience, and in practice often just leads to poking your head forwards and vocal strain. The idea of "projecting" the voice is best forgotten. Using resonators is more internal. The by-product of using the resonators is a voice which indeed extends out to the audience. Using resonators is also not to be confused with using a "head" voice and a "chest" voice. Actually you have only one voice, your voice, which ideally mixes resonance from various areas to different extents to make a rich palette of vocal colour. Resonance is about using all the parts of your instrument to make a multi-dimensional sound.[8]

Exploration 22: Exploring your resonators

In these explorations you focus on discovering resonance in the nose-eyes area. This is useful not only to promote use of the resonators, but also to clear them of any mucus, for example, after a cold.[9]

Remember to focus on function, not the sounds you are making. Remind yourself that sound is a by-product of function.

22.1 Center yourself. Remember to raise your soft palate and allow your larynx to drop. Allow your jaw to drop to open your mouth. Using the "ng" tongue position (tongue tip lightly anchored behind your lower front teeth, back of your tongue touching the back of your hard palate) breathe energetically out through your nose. Hold a finger under your nostrils. You should feel air rushing over it. Or use a feather and watch it move. When you are used to breathing energetically out through your nose and the air is moving freely, add voice (imitate a siren by sliding up and down in pitch is my suggestion). Keep the air moving all the way through the sound, right to the very end. Ideally, you will feel vibration in your nose and/or forehead.

22.2 Center yourself again, remembering to raise your soft palate. With your tongue tip resting behind your lower front teeth and the middle of your tongue touching the hard palate just behind your top teeth (on your alveolar ridge), open your mouth and do the same exploration on an "n" sound (this is probably not how you usually make an "n"). First get used to sending air through your nose this way. Then add your voice, and keep the air moving all the way through the sound. You should feel vibration in your nose.

22.3 Center yourself again. Raise your soft palate. Keep your tongue and larynx released. With your lips lightly together and your tongue resting on the floor of your mouth (but not pushing down), make an "m" sound. You should be feeling vibration in your lips and ideally also in your nose and perhaps also your forehead.

22.4 Center yourself. Keeping your lips lightly together, your soft palate raised, and your tongue and larynx released, maintain a gentle hum on one pitch. Where do you feel vibration? If you feel most of the vibration in your throat, think of sending your voice forwards and up into your face, particularly the nose-eyes area. Ideally, you will feel vibration in your lips and nasal area and even also in your forehead. Experiment with different pitches and the vibrations associated with them.

If that is going well, try counting aloud or saying a simple sentence. Think of your voice moving forwards and up into your face where you have just felt your hum.

The vexed question of vocal support

Voice coaches frequently talk about supporting the voice. What does this mean? Well, it seems to mean a range of things depending on who is talking. But the aim of all vocal support is to make speaking or singing easier, so that the voice has longevity and can do what is required of it without unnecessary strain. How to achieve that is more contentious.

If you remember exploration 10 which investigates the connection between strength and stability, you will recall that you discovered that support and therefore strength comes not from tensing up but from allowing the deep postural muscles to work well. You can be stable (but not rigid) and mobile (but not floppy) at the same time. The same goes for the voice. Support does not come from fixing the lower ribs and pushing with the abdominals. Rather it depends on free moving air flow (which is not the same as fast moving), which in turn depends on muscle elasticity and the lengthening and expanding of the whole trunk. No voice can be properly supported if the air is not flowing freely and there is too much or too little muscle tension somewhere. Support can only happen if the whole body is working well, from the feet to the crown of the head.

Here it is worth noting that in order to vocalise we do need a controlled exhale. We cannot say a sentence or sing a musical phrase with the same breathing that we use while sitting silently in front of the TV. Try it out. In order to vocalise we need to breathe out slower. Yet it is important to understand that unless we interfere, this gear shift will happen automatically whenever we have the intention of speaking or singing. It is a naturally controlled exhale. We do not have to engineer it.[10] Our breathing, larynx and communicative intention are all on the same loop. And in fact, our breathing is designed to adapt to our needs whatever we are doing. Just as we can unconsciously adapt our walking rhythm depending on terrain and intention, so we also can also unconsciously adapt our breathing rhythm depending on the demands being made on us and our intention. However, there are many ways in which we can and often do interfere with this unconscious process of adaptation. The explorations you have just done (explorations 19 and 21) and the following one are intended to help you restore your natural functioning in this respect.

Exploration 23: Exploring coordinating support

In order for the speaking apparatus to be free we need elasticity in the torso and energy in the breath flow otherwise we will necessarily compensate for what is lacking by pushing, tightening, and grasping in the throat and articulators (tongue, jaw, lips). This exploration is about coordinating release with necessary tone in the torso and controlled energy in the breath flow.[11]

23.1 Center yourself. If necessary, remind yourself of the aspects of breathing which you looked at earlier in this chapter. Go through a few breathing cycles with a controlled exhale on a hiss. Remember to:

- start the cycle on an unprepared outbreath with however much air you happen to have
- allow your ribs to move and your back to engage
- allow the exhale muscles to release after the exhale
- wait and allow the air to flow back in through your nose.

When the cycle is going well, see if you can do a lip trill on the controlled exhale instead of a hiss. This sounds like "horsey breathing", the sound that horses make after exercise, for example, but held for longer. For this the lips need to be floppy so they can vibrate as the air passes through them. At the same time, the air of the controlled exhale must flow freely and energetically.

When all is well coordinated you will notice that you actually need very little air and can sustain the lip trill for a long time with very little effort.

23.2 When that is going well, add your voice to your lip trill. You can slide up and down, invent your own tune, lip trill your favourite song, making sure to slide between the notes rather than aiming for separate notes.

When you run out of breath, wait and allow air back in through your nose. Take your time. At the beginning, in order to aid release of the exhale muscles, continue until you feel you are about to run out of breath (but don't squeeze it all out). If you are lip trilling a song, this probably means breathing unmusically. However, once that is going well, you can allow your breath to follow your phrasing rather than the other way round. This is how communication should be: your body responds to your intention without conscious intervention from you. To get you going again, remember the sequence: air – lips – voice.

Lip trills coordinate naturally controlled but energised breathing, muscle tone in the torso, and released articulators, all of which we need for easy and healthy vocalising and speaking.

Looking after Your Voice
Daily voice care routine
It is useful to have a voice care routine which you do every day, though you can, of course, add and subtract to it. It develops technique, and we do need technique in order to become vocally independent of mood and the ups and downs of life. Routine is most beneficial if you do it with awareness and curiosity. Each day can be interesting.

What follows is a suggestion for a daily routine, covering the most important aspects. If necessary, re-read and re-explore.

- Do the active resting for at least 5 minutes as often as you can.
- Center yourself in standing. Be aware of the surface under your feet, of your head balancing on the top of your spine, and your whole length between feet and head. Keep your eyes looking ahead and be aware of the space you are in, including what is behind you.
- Practise a few controlled exhales. Without any special preparation, with whatever air you happen to have, let your breath go on a hiss. Allow the air to flow back in through your nose. Repeat several times to get a cycle going. Allow your ribs and abdomen to move. Make sure you are not shrinking on the exhale; keep thinking of your lengthening spine while exhaling slowly.
- Do a few lip trills, with or without voice.

- Do a whispered "ah" a few times, remembering to raise your soft palate and let your larynx drop. Monitor tongue root tension with the ball of your thumb.
- Activate your resonance chambers with nasal consonants "ng", "n", "m".
- Hum, monitoring vibration. Direct your voice forwards and up.
- As above and when it's going well, allow your jaw to drop and sing an "ah".
- Speak a simple sentence, monitoring where you feel vibration. The further forwards and up, the better.

Other aspects of voice care

- Drink lots of water and avoid stimulants like coffee, tea, alcohol. Caffeine and alcohol tend to dehydrate the body, so if you do drink these, make sure you also drink water.
- Cut down on dairy products as they tend to lead to more mucus. If necessary, use a steam inhaler on a regular basis to clear the passageways. Add calming and cleansing oils if wished.
- Try to make breathing through your nose your default mode.
- Reflect on when and why you talk. Can you cut down on your own talking time in the classroom (or/and elsewhere)? Can you use your body and facial expression more to save your voice? Do you really need to speak now? How well do you manage silence? This, although it sounds obvious, is an important question for many teachers which it is sometimes advantageous to address. Monitor your teacher talking time and also student talking time. In most interactive teaching situations, the former should be less than the latter.

- Avoid noisy environments if you can. If you want to talk, go somewhere where that is easily possible and does not involve fighting background noise. In teaching institutions, is a quiet talking space available? If not, maybe one can be arranged.

Troubleshooting

The following includes some of teachers' most common vocal health complaints. The suggestions regarding how they might be addressed refer to the topics touched on above, so please re-read and re-explore the relevant sections, if necessary. However, this cannot replace a doctor's or other health care provider's diagnosis, and professional help might well be called for.

Hoarseness: This is often the result of trying to speak loudly wrongly. Air is pushed out in a mistaken attempt to be loud, but the total support system and the breathing muscles are not well coordinated and the throat and larynx tighten. The common response is to push even more, leading to even more tightening. This can lead to permanent voice damage.

If you find you are in this vicious circle, the first and most essential thing to do is to stop speaking and re-organise yourself. Go through the following steps:

- Make sure you are centered. Find your feet, your height, your width. Allow your head to balance on the top of your spine. Make very sure you are not poking your head forwards and collapsing at the breastbone, or pulling your head back and down, even minimally, when you breathe or speak.
- Use reflexive breathing. Remember to allow the breath to

come in by releasing the exhale muscles. And very importantly, remember to allow it out. Avoid all pushing. Remember to allow your ribs, abdomen and back to move. Keep your shoulders as uninvolved as possible. Keep the air moving as you speak.

- Make sure you are keeping your throat open, and your larynx released.
- Use your resonators. Think (don't push) your voice forwards and up onto your hard palate and into your eyes-nose area. Raise your soft palate (think of an inner smile, polite yawn with your lips lightly touching). If you are not using your resonators adequately, then you will feel your voice is trapped in your throat and you will probably push to get any volume. This will, with time, lead to hoarseness.

Too little volume: This is very similar to hoarseness.
- Again, pay attention to centering and reflexive breathing.
- Use your resonators. Think your voice forwards and up onto your hard palate and into your nose-eyes area.
- Remember to activate your soft palate, so enlarging your oral cavity.
- Open your mouth more than you are used to. This sounds obvious but needs to be practised if your habit is to speak barely opening your mouth. Practise in front of a mirror and let it feel weird.
- At the same time, it can be very helpful to imagine you are sending your voice out through your back as well as forwards. Imagine you have a 3-D voice. This also helps to prevent you poking your head forwards in an effort to reach out with your voice.

Feeling of not having enough breath and your voice is trapped: This is often caused by interfering with the exhale. If we hold in air and stop its free flow out, less air can flow in again. We feel tight in the chest and can only breathe shallowly. Our brain then registers that we do not have enough air. We are in the cycle of shallow top-up breathing. This can also give us the feeling of the voice being trapped and unable to get out. Breathing and speaking become effortful.

- Remember to center yourself. Find your feet, allow your spine to lengthen, and your head to balance on the top.
- Focus on allowing the air to leave. Do a few controlled exhales on a hiss. Let go of more air than you are perhaps used to, so keep the hiss going for longer than normal.
- Remember to allow the air to enter through release of the exhale muscles. Let your ribs and abdomen move, engage your back.
- Remember also to allow yourself enough time to breathe in, through your nose. When speaking, this often means making more use of pauses, which can only be beneficial to both you and your audience (see chapter seven on performance skills).
- A useful exercise is to practise adding an "h" sound to the beginning of a sentence, i.e. a little exhale before you speak, to get the air flowing before you add voice.

Running out of breath: Assuming there is no medical condition which compromises breathing, there are usually three main reasons for running out of breath:

- The first is an inefficient use of air while speaking, letting too much air out in a rush and with too much unused air escaping on speech sounds (breathy speaking). See below

for breathy speaking.
- The second is fixing the exhale muscles. The exhale muscles are not allowed to release fully at the end of the exhale but are fixed. As a result the inhale is compromised. In this case follow the suggestions above.
- The third is that posture is so poor that the body cannot function properly. The slump and the military position (see figure 4) are examples of this. In this case, do lots of active resting and centered standing, connecting mind to muscle.

Gasping: This is usually caused by constriction of the throat as a result of fixing muscles at the end of the exhale. (It often happens when we get nervous.) Again, follow the suggestions above, making sure you allow the inhale to happen as a result of release. Take your time. Allow your throat to stay wide and untensed. And remember your centered standing and head balance.

Cracking: Cracking of the voice is often the result of a momentary stoppage of air.
- Keep the air flowing; focus on the exhale.
- Cracking can also sometimes be caused by mucus on the vocal folds, so thin it by drinking lots of water.
- Also make sure you are mouth breathing as little as possible, as this will dry out the folds and make them produce more lubricant.

Breathy Speaking: This is caused by the edges of the vocal folds not meeting cleanly. As a result, air escapes which is not used for vocalising.
- Check (with a laryngologist) that there are no nodules on

the vocal folds which are preventing clean closure. Nodules can themselves be caused by misuse and can disappear when body and voice use improves.

• If there are no nodules you can begin to train a cleaner meeting by practising the sound "ee" (as in "me") held on any sung pitch. Try gently pressing together the thumb and forefinger of your non-dominant hand and watch that hand while vocalising. This sends a mental request for more efficient fold closure.[12]

---

[1] See Angela Caine, *The Voice Workbook. Use your Voice with Confidence* (Hodder & Stoughton, Sevenoaks, 1991), pp.28-39

[2] See Kristin Linklater, *Freeing the Natural Voice. Imagery and Art in the Practice of Voice and Language* (Nick Hern Books, London, 2006), p.281, first published in USA in 1976

[3] See Linklater, op.cit., p.171

[4] See Jane Heirich, *Voice and the Alexander Technique. Active Explorations for Speaking and Singing* (Mornum Time Press, Berkeley CA, 2005), p.85

[5] See Heirich, op.cit., p.87

[6] Thanks to Ron Murdock for this variation.

[7] See Theodore Dimon, *Your Body, Your Voice. The Key to Natural Singing and Speaking* (North Atlantic Books, Berkeley CA, 2011) p.27

[8] See Linklater, op.cit., pp.263-5

[9] Thanks to Paula Anglin for these explorations.

[10] For more on this see Theodore Dimon, op. cit., pp. 43-55. Also Angela Caine, op. cit., pp. 43-61

[11] Thanks again to Paula Anglin for this exploration.

[12] See Heirich, op.cit., pp.53-4

4

YOUR EMOTIONAL WELL-BEING

If you are distressed by anything external, the pain is not due to the thing itself, but to your estimate of it; and this you have the power to revoke at any moment. (Marcus Aurelius)

Nowadays, teachers are often considered to belong to a high stress profession, along with doctors, the police, prison officers, social workers, and air traffic controllers.[1] Although individual teachers and teaching situations vary hugely, most teachers find at least some aspects of their job stressful: an ever-growing mountain of paperwork and red tape; a looming inspection or teaching assessment; discipline and classroom management; too little time to do marking and preparation; in some cases also employment insecurity and underpayment; perhaps unsupportive or even obstructive colleagues. This is often reinforced by a feeling of being undervalued by politicians and society as a whole. Measuring their status on a scale of 1-5, British school teachers have apparently considered their own status to be well under 3.0 for the last decade, in contrast to teachers 40 years ago who gave themselves a status score of 4.3.[2]

In common parlance, stress, usually connoted negatively, generally appears to be something which exists in the outside world. We talk about a situation or person being stressful, say that we've had a lot of stress recently, or that we've been through a lot of stress. However, there are other ways of talking about stress. Some people may make a clear distinction between a situation, and the stress or strain they feel which is their reaction to that situation. Others might use it in a more general sense to refer to challenges, and see that almost all challenges will trigger positive as well as negative emotions. This view of stress recognises that it also has a positive component and without it we probably would not feel we are living satisfying lives. We need a certain buzz and excitement to save us from decaying from boredom and routine. Still others might use it more specifically to refer to the mismatch between demands made on a person and that person's own perceived ability to meet those demands.

The important point about these alternative ways of talking about stress is that the focus is shifted away from it being something which exists in the outside world, to being something which is dependent on our perception of that outside world. And, as with all matters of perception, that can vary widely. What is stressful is, then, a highly personal matter. Most commonly, however, teacher stress is used to describe the experience of emotions such as anger, frustration, anxiety, depression and nervousness resulting from some aspect of work as a teacher.[3] Interestingly and importantly this, apparently, is very often triggered by some aspect of their work being perceived as threatening to self-esteem, self-image, or well-being.[4] In other words, stress is a reaction to a perceived threat. It is, then, closely related to fear.

Exploration 24: Exploring your responses to stress
24.1 Which situations connected to teaching make you feel stressed or anxious? Do you notice any physical symptoms of stress (for example: raised heartbeat, tensing your neck, holding

your breath, clenching your jaw ...)?

24.2 Which situations connected to teaching trigger excitement or positive stress for you? What are your symptoms of this positive stress (for example: raised heartbeat, holding your breath)? What similarities do you see to the manifestations of negative stress or anxiety?

24.3 Could you imagine that the two forms of stress are on a continuum and joined by many different degrees, rather than being two discrete states? Is there a tipping point for you when positive stress becomes negative stress? Is approaching that tipping point heralded by any physical symptoms?

Understanding Stress and Anxiety

In order to get more of a handle on our own responses to perceived threat and therefore stress, it is worth understanding a little more about the psycho-physical processes which are at work. In a danger situation the part of the brain which is responsible for identifying threat, the amygdala, triggers off a neurochemical response which causes changes such as faster heartbeat, raised blood pressure, and a rush of adrenaline, a hormone which increases alertness and muscle strength. These changes are all part of self-defence responses: the body is being prepared for unusual calls on it in response to the need to deal with a perceived threat. Vertebrates have four locomotive self-defence behaviours: fight (attack), flight (run away), freeze (play dead) and submit.[5] These responses are largely stereotyped patterns which do not allow much individual variation. Once a defence behaviour is activated, our bodily sensations flood back as feedback to the brain. However, we can only become aware of what we are doing after the defence behaviour has been triggered. It is only after the neurochemical activity and stereotyped self-defence mechanisms have kicked in that we can become aware of feeling anxious, reflect on it, and give it a name. It is only then that the mind can interpret the body's feedback as fear, rationalise, override behaviours, and make conscious choices. This is in fact a survival mechanism. It cuts out conscious decision making processes, because they take too long in a real danger situation where split seconds can make the difference between life and death. This process is intended to keep us alive in genuinely dangerous situations. However, for most of us, what we experience as anxiety or stress in our everyday lives is not in response to truly life-threatening situations. Something has gone wrong.

Self-Defence gone Awry
In order to get some insight into this, it is useful to bear a few things in mind:

Firstly, the amygdala appraises stimuli and categorises them as to how threatening they are. However, it is not rational or objective in its assessments. If we are already tense then our amygdala is more likely to perceive a stimulus as a threat. We are in a vicious circle of ever-escalating tension and over-reaction.

Secondly, the amygdala learns. If it has previously classed a stimulus as a threat, it is likely to do so again, even if, objectively seen, that stimulus is harmless. With increasing everyday levels of tension, ever more stimuli are seen as harmful.

Thirdly, stress hormones such as adrenaline are beneficial and help the body cope in the short term. If, however, they are produced over a longer period of time they can have harmful effects such as impaired memory, heart disease, high blood pressure, a weakened immune system.

Fourthly, locomotive defence patterns of fight, flight, freeze, and submit, if practised in the long term, lead to lasting changes in muscle tone which compromise how we move. We become tenser, more contracted and compressed as a matter of everyday living. As this way of being becomes a habit, we believe that it is "normal" and "natural". We develop a faulty sensory awareness.

Fifthly, by becoming habituated to these defence behaviours we are out of balance and out of touch with ourselves, other people, and our environment. We can easily misjudge stimuli, either giving them too little or too much significance. We can narrow our field of awareness, focusing on one sensation while being oblivious to others. We fuel our own imbalance.

And sixthly, Western culture, which promotes immediate personal happiness as the unquestioned goal of life, tends to have little tolerance for discomfort. Emotional discomfort is immediately and simplistically classed as "bad" and to be avoided. This means we find it hard to accept discomfort with equanimity. Something slightly unpleasant happens and we are already primed to go into defence mode. However, perhaps we need to realise that a certain amount of discomfort is part of life. It is not a threat, and need not trigger defence reactions. If we can do that, we have more hope of regaining our balance and keeping a clear head so that we can give ourselves more choice about how we respond to the challenges life throws in our path.[6]

The Psycho-Physical Approach

Although it is often a highly personal matter whether a certain situation triggers stress, that is, is perceived as threatening or not, it seems to be the case that when we do feel threatened, we all very largely share the same physical symptoms. We tense up and become narrower and shorter, our heart beat rises, we tend to hold our breath, clench our jaw. We embody anxiety. Our bodily state is an emotional one and vice versa. Yet, of course, none of these symptoms promotes a successful teaching or learning experience. So what can we do about them?

Well, there are two possible, complementary, approaches. On the one hand, we could work from the inside to the outside, that is, approach the issue from a more psychological point of view. We might consider what precisely we are reacting to, what in our past has made us susceptible to this particular stress/anxiety trigger, how we might reframe it, and consider a host of other issues, all with the goal of promoting our own emotional and physical well-being. On the other hand, we can also take the outside to inside approach, based on the insight that, because we are psycho-physical beings, body as well as mind, gaining more control over our physical responses does actually help us to gain more control over how we think and feel. The body affects the mind, just as much as the mind affects the body.

Of course, the idea that changing how we behave is one of the most effective ways of changing how we think and feel is a cornerstone of behaviour therapies. If you can't make it, fake it, as the saying goes. And the important point is that faking it does in fact help you to make it. A simple example might be the experience that if you make the effort to smile even though you are feeling a bit down, you do actually begin to feel a bit more cheerful. Taking this further, we can recognise that if we are habitually physically tense, we are more likely to have tension-inducing beliefs. Conversely, if we are physically more relaxed, we have a better chance of meeting life's challenges in a more relaxed manner. And, of course, vice versa: our attitudes will find their embodiment in our muscle tension. Effecting a change in one will effect a change in the other. For this reason, if we can gain more control over the physical tensions of stress and anxiety, we stand a better chance of coming back to balance, both physically and emotionally.

In addition, by coming to a greater sense of inner calm, we will be in a better position to make any possible changes to our external situation which will help us avoid feeling threatened in the first place. This might, for example, include asking for possible institutional changes, learning to delegate, to be assertive without being aggressive, to say no, to prioritise and manage time better, and to be kinder in our demands and expectations of ourselves. It also includes a healthy private life: healthy nutrition, taking enough exercise, regular sleep patterns, and cultivating relationships and activities outside work.

Gaining Control

So how can we acquire more control over our embodiment of perceived threat? Well, simply but very powerfully, we can again apply the basic principles and skills we looked at in the previous chapters. So, for example, we can remember to lengthen our spine when stress wants us to shorten; we can remember to find our feet and good contact to the floor when stress want us to lose our balance; we can remember to breathe out when stress wants us to hold our breath; we can be aware of our peripheral vision when stress wants us to go into tunnel vision; we can remember to release our neck muscles when stress wants us to tighten them. We might well be remembering all of this with a pounding heart and sweaty palms, but by virtue of remembering and refusing to succumb completely to the embodiment of anxiety, we are gaining more control and will probably notice that with time the heartbeat quietens and the sweat diminishes.

In this regard it is important, however, to realise that we are not after eradicating all nervousness irrespective of context. In some situations, for example an important presentation, job interview, stage performance, we want the beneficial effects of adrenaline (greater alertness, muscle strength) in order to perform at our best. In other words, we want neither to exterminate the butterflies in our stomachs nor to allow them to flutter madly around; we want to get them to fly in formation. Having technique is essential here, and practising it is, too. We are concerned here with psycho-physical skills which need to be learnt and practised, and the more we hone those skills, the more we can benefit from them and have them at our fingertips when we need them.

Exploring active resting (exploration 5) on a daily basis is very helpful here. In addition to all its other benefits, active resting is also active stress prevention and management. And once again: this is an excellent practice situation which allows you to reinforce that positive connection between mind and muscle which is the foundation of conscious control. Remember to allow:
- yourself to become aware of where you have contact with your support (probably the floor)
- your weight to trickle down into the support
- your head and tailbone to swim away from each other

- your shoulders to swim away from each other
- your limbs to extend out, away from your torso
- your heels to go down into the floor and your feet to lengthen and widen
- your breath to flow freely through your nose

Remember these are energised thoughts, not actions. Try to remain on the level of thinking rather than doing. Observe with kindness and curiosity. If you notice yourself trying to do any of the thoughts, just say no to yourself (withhold consent) and go back to the thinking.

The Power of Pausing

Another useful stress-management skill which you began to explore in chapter one is to learn to put in a pause between a stimulus and your reaction to that stimulus. This helps you to choose how you want to react to external triggers and gives you the chance to say "no" to unhelpful, automatic reactions. By putting in even a momentary pause you can give yourself time to choose. This is highly applicable to stress reduction and prevention. That pause gives you the chance to stop habitual responses to a stimulus which has hitherto triggered stress, center yourself, and then to choose a perhaps new reaction. (Perhaps re-visit exploration 4.)

The magic formula is: PAUSE …. CENTER … ACT/REACT

PAUSE and stop habitual reactions to the anxiety trigger. This might mean: stopping yourself holding your breath; stopping yourself shrinking in stature; stopping yourself unnecessarily tensing your jaw, neck or any other part of yourself.

It might also mean stopping yourself agreeing to take on more tasks you don't really want to do (if that is your habit);

stopping yourself accepting others' expectations of you (if that is your habit); stopping yourself putting something off yet again (if that is your habit); stopping yourself trying to do too much in too little time (if that is your habit).

Obviously it is helpful to have an idea about which of your habits is tripping you up. Talking to close colleagues or friends can be very useful here as it is sometimes difficult to get the necessary clarity ourselves.

CENTER yourself. The more you practise centering in your everyday life, the easier it will be in situations you find more challenging. If you are centered and physically balanced you are much more likely to be emotionally and mentally balanced. Your attention can move more easily between yourself and the people you are engaging with, enabling you to attend to both your own and others' needs.

Remember to breathe out to counteract any tendency to hold your breath. This will allow the free flow of oxygen supply to your brain.

Remember to extend your personal space all around you; do not allow yourself to be trapped in frontal awareness only (this is completely independent of the room set-up).

ACT/REACT while maintaining your centering thoughts. Respond to your colleague who is asking you to do something you don't want to do, deal with what needs to be done, while at the same time thinking, for example, of your good contact with the floor, your spine lengthening, and your head balancing on the top of your spine.

The ability to think in activity in this way is the secret to moving through life with greater ease. And as with all skills, practice is the key. Use everyday life as your practice ground. The more you do it, the easier it will become, and the faster you will be able to go through the process of: pause, center, act/react.

Constructive Disassociation: Getting another Perspective
The ability to pause and withhold consent to habitual response is also at the root of a constructive use of disassociation. Disassociation, when used constructively, is not about going into denial or maintaining an emotional detachment to the world. It is simply a tool to help you get a liberating distance to what is going on around you, to take a step backwards and reconsider. Put simply, it can be a healthy reminder not to take everything in life personally. As a result it can help to reduce perceptions of threat and therefore stress.

The skill lies in knowing that we can move freely on the spectrum from association to disassociation and back again, in tune to changes in ourselves and our circumstances. Both positions of association and disassociation, when they become extremes or habits, lead us to become fixed and rigid, both mentally and muscularly. We either over-react to or are oblivious to impulses in ourselves and in the world outside. Both habits trap us and deprive us of freedom. The goal is to be able to choose the quality of our response to a stimulus, that is, whether we respond with ease or with unnecessary tension. The following explorations are intended to help you to play with that element of choice. They will help you manage stress, or even better, avoid it in the first place.

Exploration 25: Exploring coming to quiet

25.1 You need a partner for this.

Step 1
Stand opposite each other at a comfortable distance. One of you (A) holds a soft ball (so soft that there need be no fear of getting hurt or damaging fittings and fixtures). Both should be centering during this exploration.

Step 2
A goes through the motions of throwing the ball to their partner (B) but does not throw it, and B knows it will not be thrown.

Step 3
B disassociates from A's actions. If necessary, B can look away from A at the beginning. Be patient. B tries to be aware of even tiny muscular responses to A.
B monitors those smaller areas which often store unnecessary tension, for example: the jaw; tongue root; the face particularly around the eyes; fingers and particularly thumbs; toes. Monitor the breathing. Ideally, with time there is absolutely no response on any level in B to what A is doing.

A can usually sense when B has really reached disassociation (clues are often in the facial muscles, eyes, breathing). Generally, a sense of calm and space prevails for both B and A.

Step 4
Talk about your observations to each other. This also includes A's responses to this exploration. Change roles.

25.2 If that is going well, you can repeat the exploration, but this time B does not know whether A will throw the ball or not. Sometimes A will throw, sometimes not. Agree in advance a procedure for retrieving the ball. Again both A and B monitor their

responses. B is aiming for complete disassociation from A's actions.
Exchange observations and change roles.

Many people discover that the following exploration helps them get a useful distance to stressful situations by helping them realise that different narratives can be given to the same situation depending on perceptual position. What we experience as fact might (in fact) be opinion. This insight can help you see your own narrative as just one of several possible ones. Realising this can help you let go of some of the threatening emotional baggage attached to that situation.

Exploration 26: Exploring perceptual positions
26.1 This exploration helps you to get a different perspective when needed. In this exploration, you can either imagine you are talking to a benevolent partner or really do so.[7]

Think of a teaching situation which makes you moderately stressed, but do not choose anything too extreme. In practice it is precisely the smaller, recurrent annoyances which can stress us most. The real emergencies are, thankfully, rare and most of us then rise to the occasion. It's the daily grind that gets us down most.
Notice what imagining that situation does to you. What body changes do you notice?

First perceptual position:
Describe that situation to yourself or your partner from the first person perspective, using "I": I feel, I am, I have. Describe what you can see, hear, taste, sense. Describe your feelings, thoughts. This is your perception of the situation and is the perspective most of us spend most of our lives in; we see things through our own eyes.

Your Emotional Well-Being

Second perceptual position:
Describe the same situation now using the third person singular (she/he) from the viewpoint of your audience (students, colleagues): She/he walks in, says, does, etc. Put yourself in your audience's position; what do you see, experience? How might you, a member of the audience, feel?

Third perceptual position:
Now imagine a benevolent observer is standing at the door and looking at the situation and the people interacting. This is the detached position of the coach. How would that observer describe the situation, using the third person singular and plural (he/she, they)? How would that observer describe the ways the people are interacting in this situation?

Learning to be your own coach can be very useful. It can help you disentangle yourself from the confines of the first position and get a wider perspective. It can help you see where you and your audience are meeting and where you are not, and what you might do to change things. The following exploration promotes these stress management skills.

Exploration 27: Exploring being your own stress management coach

27.1 This exploration helps you work on a particular situation which causes you moderate stress or anxiety (but again don't choose anything too extreme).
You can do this one on your own.[8]

Step 1
Imagine yourself somewhere you feel comfortable and unthreatened: Where are you? What time of day is it? What are you doing? What can you see? Hear? Smell? Touch? Really put yourself in that place of ease.

In that situation observe your:
breathing: its speed, depth, audibility
visual field: its breadth, clarity
posture: your contact with supporting surfaces; your alignment; any areas of unnecessary habitual tension, for example in your neck, shoulders, jaw
personal space: its felt size
self-belief: what are your internal voices saying? Are they supportive or nagging?
Make notes afterwards if you like.

Step 2
Imagine yourself in the moderate anxiety state you have chosen to investigate: Where are you? What time of day is it? What are you doing? What can you see? Hear? Smell? Touch?

Slowly go through the checklist above (breathing, visual field, posture, personal space, self-belief), observing yourself in that situation. Again, make notes afterwards if you like.

Step 3
Imagine yourself in your emotionally comfortable state watching the moderately stressed you as if on a TV screen to which you hold the remote control in your hand.

Now slowly go through the checklist above again, point for point (breathing, visual field, posture, personal space, self-belief) transferring, for example, the breathing of the comfortable you to the moderately anxious you on the TV. You might like really to move a finger as if using the on-off switch of the imaginary remote control.

So, for example, first turn off the moderately anxious you on your mental TV screen, transfer the breathing of the comfortable you to the anxious you, turn on the TV and let it run for a while with your easy breathing.

Then turn off the TV, transfer the visual field of the comfortable you to the moderately anxious you, turn on the TV, let it run for a while with both the breathing and visual field of the comfortable you, etc.

When you have gone through all the points, let the edited and adapted film run again on your mental TV set.

You might find it difficult to go through all the points, or one might be easier to transfer than another. But you will probably find that changing even only one aspect will make a big difference to how you feel and will have a knock-on effect for all the other aspects.

In Search of Tranquillity

If we can regularly practise stopping, centering, and constructive disassociation we are on the path to the freedom to choose. Of course, we cannot always choose which stimuli we are confronted with nor probably choose which of those stimuli tend to put us wrong and trigger feelings of threat, but we can learn to give ourselves at least some choice as to how we respond. This is what the skill of good self-management or self-use is all about. We can, for example, choose how we respond to feelings of threat. We can choose whether we turn them into sources of stress or not. And interestingly, believing that we have choice does in itself often bring about a change in whether we perceive something as threatening or not. Gradually, we notice that what used to upset us just does not upset us as much anymore. We have brought more tranquillity into our lives.

This ability to choose our responses is, according to the

Austrian psychiatrist and concentration camp survivor, Viktor Frankl, not only the path to tranquillity but to more. How we choose to respond to difficult events and circumstances, what Frankl calls attitude, is in itself one of the ways we can make life meaningful and worth living.[9] Learning to choose our responses to perceived threat is part, then, of choosing an attitude towards life as a whole and the challenges it presents us with, and therefore part and parcel of the meaning we give our lives. We can either choose responses which promote our well-being and give life a benevolent face, or ones which do not. It is in our hands.

---

[1] See Chris Kyriacou, *Stress-busting for Teachers* (Stanley Thornes Publishers, Cheltenham, 2000), p.14

[2] See Linda Hargreaves et al., *The Status of Teachers and the Teaching Profession in England. Views from Inside and Outside the Profession*, Research Report RR831A (Department for Education and Skills, 2007), cited in Julian Baggini and Antonia Macaro, *The Shrink and the Sage. A Guide to Living* (Icon books, London, 2012), p.141

[3] See Kyriacou, op.cit., p.5

[4] See Kyriacou, op.cit., p.9

[5] See Missy Vineyard, *How you Stand, how you Move, how you Live. Learning the Alexander Technique to explore your Mind-Body Connection and achieve Self-Mastery* (Marlowe, New York, 2007), p.74

[6] See Vineyard, op.cit., pp.81-90

[7] See Alan Mars, *Confidence Tricks. Presenter* (2013), pp.56-59

[8] I am grateful to Alan Mars for this exploration.

[9] See Viktor Frankl, *Man's Search for Meaning* (Rider, London, 2004), p.115. First published in German in 1946.

PART TWO

MAKING MORE OF YOURSELF

Make the most of yourself, for that is all there is of you.
(Ralph Waldo Emerson)

5

DEVELOPING YOUR SPEAKING SKILLS

Speak the speech, I pray you ... trippingly on the tongue.
(William Shakespeare)

Along with the self-care skills that we have already looked at, speaking skills are amongst the basic tools of any teacher's toolbox. Speech is, after all, the predominant mode of communication in the classroom. This means that in addition to the vocal aspects dealt with in chapter three, teachers need to be able to use their speaking apparatus well. In the classroom easy intelligibility and audibility are essential. And for that to happen, the tongue, lips and jaw need to be free and responsive to the speaker's intention. Habits of speaking which hinder that freedom need to be relinquished. Perhaps new, better habits will need to be formed. All teachers and presenters need to be skilful speakers and that means that all need to have conscious control over their speech habits.

Speaking and Habit

Acquiring language as a child and thereby being inducted into a language community is one of the most fundamental forms of conditioning we can experience. How we perceive and interact with the world around us is to a large degree mediated through language and culture. In addition, although all humans share the same vocal anatomy and physiology, how we learn to use our apparatus varies tremendously according to language. This means that not only does which language we speak as children affect how we think, it also affects how we use our muscles. Each language variant has its own interior vowel shapes and use of consonant articulators which demand a certain use of the tongue, lips, jaw and also facial muscles. On top of that, each of us learns individualised habits of speaking and ways of using (or misusing) our speaking apparatus. These habits can sit very deep indeed.

In addition to learning a way of thinking and making sounds, we also learn a way of using our whole body to communicate. We learn to speak not only with words but also with facial expression, eye contact, gesture, posture, non-verbal sounds. These all belong to our early conditioning. Later, we learn, and let's hope also hone, further communication skills (however rudimentary) such as the use of volume, pace, pause, intonation, and also dialogic skills such as the use of register, softeners, back-channelling, and rules governing turn-taking, for instance. Much of this, however, happens largely subconsciously and we only notice the existence of these elements when something does not fit in with dominant cultural norms. What we say, how we say it, the sounds we make, the non-verbal language we use - all of these are cornerstones of our cultural identity.

Speaking and Cultural Values
Despite the huge room for individual variation in how we speak, cultural categories such as gender, class, age, and region, all play their important parts in constructing a language community, and how we speak is to a considerable extent an embodiment of that community's values. For example, the phrase "the stiff upper lip", applied primarily although not exclusively to men, is not merely a metaphor for a set of values

once (and for some perhaps still) admired by the British middle and upper classes. It was and is a muscular reality. Emotional repression does indeed lead to a tension and tightening in the upper lip and to the clipped tones associated with it. However, now that in modern Britain emotional restraint has lost some of its value, the stiff upper lip is dying out and new muscle uses and speech norms are becoming dominant. In fact, we seem to find almost the opposite taking over: a general lack of muscle tone in the face and extremely sluggish articulators and as a result, pulled down voices and the disappearance of consonants. Again, this seems to apply particularly to men. The stiff upper lip might be dying out, but it seems that the British male is still cautious in his communication. This might be seen in contrast to, say, the Italian love of "putting on a show". This has positive value in Italy but interestingly, a negative connotation in Britain where attracting attention to yourself, variously labelled "making a fuss, showing off, making a scene, making a spectacle of yourself" is, on the whole, still frowned upon. Thus Italians are much more likely to have facial muscle tone, a free jaw, a mobile face, open gestures, and use eye contact as part of the show. Their communication is altogether more energised and "out there" than the restrained, self-effacing communication of their British counterparts.

Changing Speech Habits

In view of their early origins and the cultural and emotional baggage attached to them, we are taking on a huge task when we try to gain conscious control over our speech habits. This is true whether we are changing habits in our mother tongue or learning to speak a foreign language. Of course, the latter is usually the more extreme case. When we learn to speak a foreign language we are confronted with an unfamiliar set of language rules, conventions, and cultural values, that is, with unfamiliar ways of thinking and constructing meaning. In addition, we are confronted with an unfamiliar body use. We need to make different sounds, use different gestures, use our face or eyes differently, perhaps even stand differently from the ways we are used to. We need to enter with our whole selves into a new communicative world. This is a huge challenge.

Yet whether we are speaking a foreign language or seeking to change our speech habits in our mother tongue, in both cases we need to relinquish habits. We do not start from neutral. Mind and body have already been programmed. We are not a *tabula rasa*, as perhaps very young, pre-verbal children are. We have already learnt a language-specific mind and muscle use, and the more monolingual we are, the more that use has become entrenched and it becomes increasingly difficult to use our mind and muscles in the often subtly different ways demanded by new speech habits.

The embodiment of language, the integration of the whole self when speaking, is, however, the key to easy speaking and communication. Speakers of English as a foreign language sometimes come to me asking for help in accent reduction so that they can be more easily understood. In my experience the problem lies not so much with the accent, that is with specific sounds they are making, as with the total communicative gesture. This includes aspects such as voice quality, tempo, use of pause, but also general tension habits which impede the desire to communicate and muddle the thinking. Communication is not just a matter of "correct" language choices and making specific sounds according to some native speaker model. (And which model to choose is itself a huge and very vexed question.) It is far more a matter of using the whole self to promote communication. In my experience, the more centering, breathing, voicing, speaking, and communicative intention become one, the less work is needed on specific phonemes. So, for example, instead of doing targeted pronunciation work, we will often work on total functioning (as covered in the preceding chapters of this book), and intelligibility automatically increases.

Coming back to Neutral
The fundamental point is that the act of speaking is a psycho-physical activity which is largely governed by habit. In order to learn new habits, either in our mother tongue or in a foreign language, we have to be able to withhold consent to old habits, while of course being able to return to them whenever we choose. We need to clear the decks first, rather than skipping that step and superimposing unfamiliar muscle use straight onto already existing language-specific tensions. In other words, we first need to be able to come back to neutral.

Through learning to release habitual tensions which govern how we use our speaking apparatus, we can clear the ground for new use. Being able to come back to neutral is altogether a highly useful skill and largely what the work presented in this book is all about. It means being able to allow the body-mind to do its work without interference from unhelpful habits of mind and muscle. However, as has already been stressed in previous chapters, we do need to be very clear here that this is not the same thing as going floppy. It is simply about saying "no" to unnecessary tension. This demands clarity of thinking

Developing Your Speaking Skills

and a strong connection between mind and muscle. In practice, however, if we are unused to this kind of work, we often need to go through a process of consciously connecting with and activating body parts before we can think about releasing unnecessary tensions and coming back to neutral.

The following information and explorations are intended to help you:
- start to discover your speaking apparatus (jaw, lips, tongue)
- activate it where necessary
- experiment with withholding consent to habitual use.

For all the following explorations you, of course, need to remember to apply what you explored in the previous chapters. If necessary, re-read and re-explore.

Coming back to Neutral: Your Jaw

Your jaw is the moveable bone into which your lower teeth are inserted. It is not where your upper teeth are, whatever any language, which talks of an upper and a lower jaw, might suggest. Your upper teeth are fixed in bone which is part of your skull. This is important to realise. If you try to open your mouth crocodile-fashion by moving the so-called upper jaw, then you have to pull your head back and down. This can easily lead to collapse in the torso and have detrimental effects on your breathing, amongst other things.

Your jaw is suspended from your skull by slotting into a groove just in front of your ears. This is the temporomandibular joint (TMJ). Open your mouth a little and put the first two fingers of each hand on your skull just in front of each ear. Then slowly close and open your mouth. You should feel your jaw moving. The jaw is raised and the mouth held shut by two sets of strong muscles: temporalis and masseter. To find these, clench your teeth. The bulge you will feel with the palms of your hands at your temples is the temporalis and the bulge at your cheeks is the masseter muscles. (A third, smaller, muscle the medial pterygoid which lies under the masseter also helps to close the jaw.) Temporalis and masseter are powerful, vertical muscles which are designed to be used for biting and chewing, but not for speaking. We do not need to "chew our words". When these muscles are released, gravity will allow the jaw to fall and the mouth to open. (Only one set of small muscles, the lateral pterygoid, helps to open the jaw, otherwise all the work is done by gravity.) A free jaw, that is, one which is in neutral, can hang to a certain extent but does not gape. We are not after a huge opening, but after release of the jaw.

In order to go back to neutral we need to be able to release the jaw. However, one of our strongest emotional-muscular defence systems is in the jaw muscles. We clench the jaw to show determination and resilience and to hide softer emotions. We bite back our words and emotions. To be "slack-jawed" is, in the English-speaking world at least, a term of denigration. The result is that many of us store a lot of unhelpful tension in the jaw muscles which interferes with voice and speech, largely by compromising the space in the oral cavity. A free jaw is essential for clear, easy speaking.

Exploration 28: Exploring your jaw
28.1 Notice how often you clench your jaw in everyday life. Notice which situations trigger clenching. Do you tighten your jaw while you speak? Observe yourself in a mirror.

When you catch yourself clenching, stop it. With your lips lightly together, allow your jaw to drop. Ask temporalis and masseter to release and lengthen.

At the same time think of your face widening at the cheekbones and of making an inner smile which reaches your eyes, but be careful to allow your thoughts to speak to your muscles rather than manufacturing an external smile. We do not want a false smile with the lips alone.

By thinking of a smile we are, amongst other things, toning the facial muscles we use to smile and laugh. In contrast to the verticality of temporalis and masseter, these fan up and out from the lips to the cheeks and eyes. Thus a free jaw, that is a jaw in neutral, does not mean walking around with a hangdog expression. A free jaw means a lively, toned, widening at the cheekbones face, with engaged eyes and a jaw which is ready to be used to do whatever our communicative intention wants it to do.

Exploration 29: Exploring freeing your jaw

29.1 You can support releasing temporalis and masseter, the two sets of muscles which many of us habitually overuse, with this exploration.

Center yourself. Bring your fingertips up to your forehead. Let your jaw drop while keeping your lips together. Massage gently over your temples and cheeks.

Then pressing quite firmly into your cheeks with the balls of your hands, stroke down over your cheeks and jaw and allow your jaw to go down with your hands, so your lips part and your mouth opens, slack-jawed.

Do this several times.

29.2 When you work on releasing your jaw you will probably want to yawn. Go ahead, do it. Relish yawning. Cultivate it. It nourishes your brain and body by increasing oxygen intake and encourages jaw release.

Coming back to Neutral: Your Lips

We use our lips for all sorts of activities: eating, drinking, kissing, playing wind instruments, singing, sucking, whistling ... And of course, we use them for speaking. It is important to know, however, that your lips are part of your facial muscles and are larger than you think they are; they are not just the lipstick lips. They are in fact big and fat and spread up to the base of your nose and down to your gums.[1] Your lips are intended to move but often they are habitually tense and tight (pursed lips). If this is the case it will impede your ability to move them to make consonants and shape vowels. The freedom of both lips to move easily is essential to clear and lively articulation and means you do not have to use the jaw unnecessarily in order to compensate. If one lip is stiff – for example, the proverbial stiff upper lip – the lower one will have to do extra work and will probably have to get extra help from your jaw. This means you will not be able to come back to neutral in the lips or jaw.

Exploration 30: Exploring your lips

30.1 What shapes can you make with your fat movement lips? Feel and see what you can do with them. Trumpet your lips, make a snout with your lips and see how much of your face moves, grin with them, purse them. Notice how big they are and how your lipstick lips just move with your larger movement lips.

30.2 Do lip trills (see exploration 23). These will energise your lips but still keep them free.
If you have difficulty with this, persevere. You can probably help

yourself by giving yourself a facelift. With your fingers gently fan your skin up and out to the sides away from your upper lip. Your fingers are supporting the freedom of your jaw (see above). A free jaw enables the lips and tongue to be free and vice versa.[2]

30.3 Do lots of humming. Relish the vibrations you can feel in your lips. Let vibrations spread through your face, up your nose, through your forehead, to the back of your skull, up out of the top of your head. Remember to raise your soft palate, and to keep your tongue free and your larynx dropped but not pushed down.

Coming back to Neutral: Your Tongue

Your tongue is a large, strong muscle which can be very nimble when it is free. However, like other muscles, it can also be habitually unduly tensed; in that case we are quite literally tongue-tied. Undue tension in the tongue – and the tongue is very sensitive to emotional triggers – will lead, for example, to the tongue bunching up, being pulled back and down into the throat, or pushed down on the floor of the mouth. These contractions change the shape of the oral cavity and interfere with voice quality and articulation. In addition, the tongue root connects to the larynx (via the hyoid bone). Any undue tension in the tongue will impair the working of the larynx. In short: your tongue plays an important part in your harmonious functioning. Ideally, we want a free tongue which can be called on to respond to the communicative intention with the contractions in the right parts of the tongue, keeping the tongue root at all times free. This is a tongue which has come back to neutral and is ready for any action demanded of it.

Exploration 31: Exploring releasing your tongue
31.1 Open wide your mouth and take a look at your tongue with

the help of a mirror. Remember that what you can see is only a small part of it; it extends further down your throat. See this in your mind's eye. Notice whether your tongue moves involuntarily; whether it bunches up at the back; is hollowed in the middle. Does it seem to have a life of its own which you were largely unaware of?

Notice what your habitual resting place for your tongue is. We often clamp it to the roof or push it down onto the floor of the mouth, particularly when concentrating. The ideal resting place is flat on the floor of the mouth with the tip lightly behind the lower front teeth where they meet the gum. Do not push it down. Pushing will unduly depress the larynx and impede breathing and voice production.

31.2 Activate your tongue. Stretch it. Place the tip behind your lower front teeth and stick your tongue out keeping the tip in place. The middle of your tongue will bulge out. This gives a greater stretch than simply sticking the tip of your tongue out.

31.3 Take your tongue to the gym; it's a muscle which wants to be used and exercised.

Run the tip of your tongue over the outside of your upper and lower teeth, from right to left and back again. Do the same with the inside of your teeth. Stick your tongue out, move from side to side, in and out. Turn it up towards your nose and down towards your chin.

31.4 Release the root of your tongue. Think of it lengthening out of your throat. Make several raspberries: the tip of your floppy, released tongue is outside and resting against your floppy, released lower lip. Your floppy, released upper lip rests on your tongue and you energetically blow air out.

If this is going well, vocalise while making a raspberry. Notice if the raspberries become more difficult. If so, this is probably an indication that you have the habit of tensing your tongue root when vocalising. Making raspberries is useful in that it checks that the tongue root is free.

31.5 Now sit or stand centered with the ball of your thumb pressing lightly upwards under the fleshy part of your jaw. Let your jaw drop and say "ha". You should not feel any pressing down on your thumb as you say this. If you do you probably have the habit of tensing your tongue root while speaking. Stop and release your tongue. Think of it lengthening and going forwards. It can lightly rest on the floor of your mouth and is not needed to make this sound.

Your tongue and vowels: Vowels carry emotional content, whereas consonants give form and structure to what we say. They are made as the sound waves are moulded into different shapes by the tongue and to a lesser extent the lips.[3] The important thing to realise is that vowels are largely formed or shaped internally, and it is their individual shape which gives each vowel its clear identity. This clarity in the vowels is essential for easy intelligibility. For this reason it is important to come to grips with internal vowel shaping. And this means that we need to have a high degree of awareness of what we can do with the tongue. It also means that the tongue and lips need to be freely available for shaping and not limited in what they can do by habitual tensions. The following explorations aim to raise awareness of what you can do with your tongue to make some vowels.

Exploration 32: Exploring shaping vowels with your tongue

32.1 Look at figure 9.

In this exploration, your mouth is open and you have vertical interior space in your oral cavity. You are letting your breath flow.

The tip of your tongue is anchored behind your lower front teeth. Starting from the "ng" tongue position, with the hump of your tongue meeting the roof of your mouth at the back where the hard palate ends, let the hump move down slowly away from the roof towards the floor of your mouth and back up again.

Play around with this to get used to the tongue movement. Your jaw should not be involved. Your tongue tip remains lightly anchored behind your lower front teeth. (You explored this also in exploration 21.2)

Then experiment with voicing and making vowels. The focus is still on the tongue position; the lips are merely adding the final shaping touch. Try to say the vowels found in, for example, "food", "oh", "far". Do each sound individually. If that is going well, slide from one to the other, as your tongue moves from top to bottom. Your tongue needs to lose touch with the roof of your mouth only minimally to make the vowel sound in "food". Your tongue tip stays anchored. Think of your tongue being quite narrow.

32.2 Look at figure 10.

Do the same exploration starting from the "n" tongue position, with your tongue tip behind your lower front teeth and the middle of your tongue on the alveolar ridge. (This might not the way you usually make an "n".)

Explore tongue movement. First move your tongue slowly from top to bottom and back again, keeping the tongue tip lightly anchored behind your lower front teeth. Then say the vowels in, for example, "he", and "hay". Start from the "n" position and let your tongue move from top to bottom, while your tongue tip stays anchored.

Keep the air flowing over your tongue, in the space between your elastic soft palate and tongue.[4]

Developing Your Speaking Skills

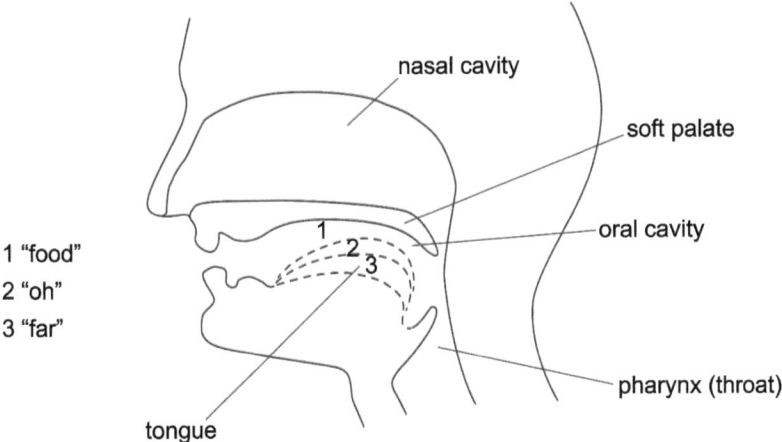

Figure 9: Internal vowel shaping starting from the "ng" tongue position

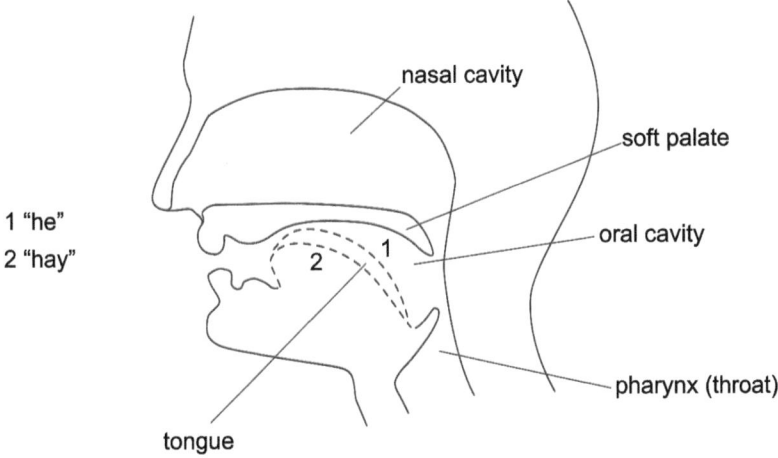

Figure 10: Internal vowel shaping starting from the "n" tongue position

Your tongue and consonants: Consonants are what gives our sound structure and turns it into recognisable speech. Without them, we would just have a stream of vowel sounds. They are made by two articulating surfaces meeting or almost meeting and in this way modifying or disturbing the sound waves. Articulating surfaces include: the lips, the tip of the tongue, the teeth, the alveolar ridge, to name a few.

Exploration 33: Exploring consonants
33.1 Experiment with consonants which are formed by part of the tongue meeting a surface (part of the roof of your mouth, your front teeth) for example: "t", "d", "k", "g", "l", "r", voiced "th" (as in "then") and unvoiced "th" (as in "thin"). Notice which part of your tongue is meeting which surface.
Be very aware if you want to compensate for a not completely mobile tongue by using your jaw. If necessary, hold your jaw in your hands to stabilise it. For economy and clarity of articulation, your tongue should be doing most of the moving. Your jaw is clumsy compared to your tongue.

Being aware of how to shape vowels and use consonants greatly promotes intelligibility which in turn promotes communication. If people can understand you easily, you are more likely to be taken seriously and seen to have authority. In addition, your whole voice increases in resonance, with all the attendant benefits of greater expressivity, carrying power, and impact. Interestingly, breathing often also improves when attention is paid to internal vowel shaping.

Tongue twisters: As the name suggests, these are little rhymes which encourage your tongue to be nimble otherwise it will twist itself into a knot. The following are just a few of the most familiar tongue twisters in English, each focusing on a particular sound or sounds.

Exploration 34: Exploring tongue twisters

Remember to stay centered. Start slowly and work up speed. Keep your jaw as released as possible, while your tongue and lips are agile. Use them more than you would in ordinary speech; they need to be energised and woken up. Choose and shape each word. The chin musculature is part of your lips, not to be confused with jaw movement. Remember to use resonators and an elastic soft palate.

Each rhyme tells a little story. Who is it about? Where did it happen? What happened? Really tell the story. Imagine you are reciting these to a group of intelligent children who are a little hard of hearing. They will be lip reading even more than we all anyway do, even those of us who do not have any hearing impediment.

34.1 Peter Piper picked a peck of pickled pepper.
Did Peter Piper pick a peck of pickled pepper?
If Peter Piper picked a peck of pickled pepper,
Where's the peck of pickled pepper
Peter Piper picked?

34.2 The Leith police dismisseth us, I'm thankful sir to say,
The Leith police dismisseth us, they thought we sought to stay,
The Leith police dismisseth us, we both sighed sighs apiece,
And the sigh that we sighed as we said goodbye,
Was the size of the Leith police.

34.3 A flea and fly in a flue were trapped,
So what did they do?
Said the flea to the fly let us flee,
Said the fly to the flea let us fly,
So they flew through a flaw in the flue.

Total Pattern Awareness

Spoken communication involves the whole of us. In addition to the words and grammatical structures we choose, intonation, facial expression, posture, gesture, voice quality, non-verbal sounds, use of space, how close we stand to our conversation partner are all an essential and inescapable part of every face-to-face spoken exchange. We speak with a total pattern which brings together language, voice, body, and communicative impulse. As listeners, we respond to that total pattern with our own total pattern. During a conversation a constant exchange and modification of total pattern responses takes place. These patterns are to a large degree culturally mediated, while, of course, leaving room for individual variation. Speaking well entails being aware of and being able to adopt and adapt communicative patterns appropriate to any given context or language. This means being aware of our habits and being able to step outside them, as and when we wish or need to.

For most of us, we learn a set of total patterns to a greater or lesser degree subconsciously as part of our process of socialisation. Learning to a large extent happens through copying. We are, in fact, programmed to copy. Although this is particularly true of young children, it also applies to adults. And the more skilful copycats we are, the better we learn. If as adults we want to promote our communication skills and be able to step outside habits which confine us, it is useful to train our powers of observation, listening and reproduction. If we have observed and listened well, we can usually copy well. And copying new, non-habitual total patterns can open the doors to new ways of communicating.

The objection is sometimes raised that copying entails a loss of authenticity and identity on the part of the speaker. Reproducing unfamiliar total patterns is seen as an encroachment on individuality and personal expression. This criticism is made when we are dealing with speaking in one's mother tongue, and it becomes even more acute when speaking in a foreign language. Why, learners often ask, should a foreign language speaker aim to speak like a native, right down to gestures, facial expression and non-verbal sounds? Why should this be the goal? Why not glory in foreignness? As long as all participants can understand and be understood, who cares if they are far from native speaker norms? And who are these often idealised "native speakers" who should be emulated anyway? Native speakers are a highly mixed bunch showing a huge amount of variation. And there is almost inevitably a lot of political baggage attached to choosing one speaker group as the model for others to copy.

All of these objections are completely valid. And at the same time they diminish what exploring speaking habits can offer. Certainly, if we regard speaking only in the light of pragmatic communication, only as a means to an end, then yes, why should we bother with expanding our repertoire of total pattern communication so long as we are intelligible? But there is the rub. Are we as easily intelligible as we might be? Or does staying within the narrow furrow of our habits force our listeners to work harder than necessary in order to understand us? We need to be able critically to appraise our habits and their usefulness. And that means we need self-awareness. And anyway, should we, as teachers, be content simply with being intelligible? Or should we be after more than that as regards our communication?

Exploring unfamiliar total patterns gives us an opportunity to step outside our habitual and well-tried ways of being and speaking. It is valuable precisely because it invites us to experiment with patterns which are different to what we are used to. It is part of developing our skill at changing and making the most of ourselves. We can see copying other people's patterns as exciting and enriching, rather than as unnecessary or even threatening. We can glory in our own individuality and identity, in our own way of doing things, and at the same time glory in learning to play with doing things differently. It is perhaps analogous to trying on new clothes in a shop. You do not have to buy the new dress and wear it every day, but it can be fun to try on something you have never worn or would never even think of wearing and just see how it feels. Sometimes we can be pleasantly surprised. But the main thing is to get used to trying things on.

Exploration 35: Exploring training total pattern awareness
If you have some knowledge of a foreign language it can be very helpful to do this exploration in that language. We are often more aware of total communicative patterns if they are not so familiar to us. If you do not know a foreign language, do it in your mother tongue.

35.1 Watch and listen to a short YouTube clip (a few minutes are quite enough) where you can see and hear people speaking your chosen language. Choose a text type where there is an element of clear gesture. A sitcom or a rousing political speech are often good.
Turn off the sound and listen with your eyes. Look at: gesture, facial expression, posture, eye contact, stillness and movement, proximity to others, use of space. Make notes. You might need to watch several times, focusing on one element at a time.
Can you still get the gist of what is being said? Is it easier to read emotion than anything else? How far does getting the gist depend on the text type, for example whether you are watching a sitcom or debate? How far is the use of the non-verbal elements typical

and predictable for that text type?

Now turn the sound on and look away. Can you imagine what gestures, facial expressions etc might be being made to fit the language? Check by looking again.

35.2 If you are feeling curious, try to imitate the total pattern of one speaker. You very likely will not sound or move like that speaker, but that is not the point. The point of copying is to make you look and listen more attentively and become more aware of what the speaker is doing and saying and how the two go together.

---

[1] See Barbara Conable, *How to learn the Alexander Technique. A Manual for Students* (Andover Press, Portland OR, 1995), p.85

[2] See Angela Caine, *The Voice Workbook. Use your Voice with Confidence* (Hodder & Stoughton, Sevenoaks, 1991), pp.71-74

[3] See Kristin Linklater, *Freeing the Natural Voice. Imagery and Art in the Practice of Voice and Language* (Nick Hern Books, London, 2006), p.17, first published in the USA in 1976.

[4] Thanks to Paula Anglin for this exploration.

6

DEVELOPING YOUR LISTENING SKILLS

I like to listen. I have learned a great deal from listening carefully. (Ernest Hemingway)

Sound is one of the most fundamental aspects of our lives. We are surrounded by a sea of sound from before we are born. In contrast to our more external eyes, our ears receive sound directly into the body via vibration. We might say that we more immediately internalise what we hear than what we see. Language has its origins in the need to communicate and that original communication was through sounds made by the human body. However, over the centuries, with writing, printing and now electronic media, the role of the ear in receiving verbal communication has increasingly diminished as the role of the eye has increased. The visual sense now tends to dominate communication in our era of information. The ear takes second place to the eye. In order to speak well we need, however, to be receptive to sound: to the sounds others make, and to the sounds we make ourselves. Listening and speaking are intimately connected. We need to reinstate the importance of the ear in communication.[1] This chapter will explore how the first principles which have guided us so far can open up how we hear and listen. It will be assumed that the ability to hear in medical terms is not an issue.

How we Hear with the Ear

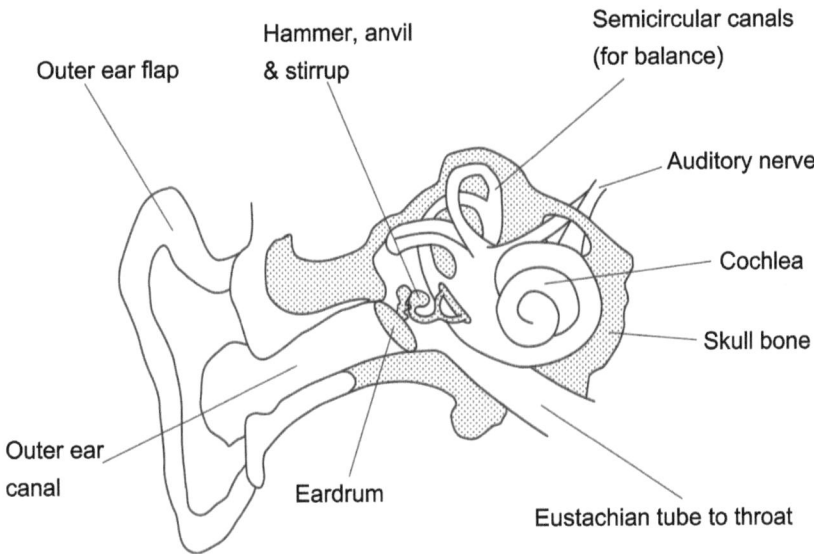

Figure 11: The ear

The human ear is a highly sensitive organ which not only enables us to hear but also to be aware of our position in space and to balance. Similar to a funnel, the outer ear collects the sound waves and transmits them through the outer ear canal to the ear drum, a membrane which vibrates in sympathy with the frequencies (pitch) and amplitudes (volume) of the sound waves.[2] These vibrations then pass through three tiny bones, the hammer, anvil, and stirrup, which in turn transmit the vibrations to the cochlea, an organ shaped like a nautilus shell or conch and filled with fluid, which is located deep in the head behind the eyes. The vibrations in the fluid of the cochlea are then converted into electrical nerve signals which are sent to the brain via the auditory nerves. In the brain the signals are selected, ordered and processed. Most of this is done subconsciously. Those sounds which have been stored in your memory bank of sounds and your brain considers to be important are recognised and you hear.[3] The human ear cannot hear all the frequencies which exist on our planet. We can hear only a small spectrum, and that spectrum often decreases with age. Yet we are surrounded by sound energy all the time.

Coming back to Auditory Neutral: Wide Focus Hearing
Auditory neutral might be considered to be wide focus hearing in contrast to narrow focus listening. It can be considered analogous to wide focus seeing in contrast to narrow focus looking. Wide focus hearing means we are open to the sounds which just happen to be in our environment at any one time. These are inevitably filtered by the brain, but we do not consciously give one sound more attention than another in an attempt to listen. Wide focus hearing is useful for bringing us back into the here and now and making us more present. It is a great antidote to mind-wandering and keeps us alert.

If we want to listen well, it is important to be able also to hear well, in the sense of being able to go into wide focus hearing and to control our habits of diminishing auditory awareness. If we can do that, then we can usually listen better. We need to be able to hear and to listen simultaneously, that is, to maintain a unified field of auditory awareness. If we go into solely narrow focus listening we will often tense up, particularly in the neck and jaw, interfere with our breathing, and generally lose connection with ourselves and our environment. It is important to keep the jaw and neck free in order to hear well. The oto-mandibular ligaments connect the mid-ear with the temporomandibular joint (TMJ). If the

Developing Your Listening Skills

movement of the TMJ is habitually restricted by overtense jaw muscles (temporalis and masseter), the mid-ear will not be able to work as well as it might.

Exploration 36: Exploring wide focus hearing

36.1 Go on a sound walk.

You can do this either alone or in a group, in an urban environment or in the countryside.

A sound walk is a walk where you move through the given soundscape. You are not focusing on any particular sounds, but instead open to whatever happens to be there.

Allow the sounds which are in the environment, that is, external sound energy, to come to you, rather than you sending your energy out to find sound.

Our ears often hear what our eyes see. Does having your eyes shut change your hearing?

How easy do you find this? Do you find you get snagged on particular sounds? Perhaps sounds you deem unpleasant or irritating? Can you hear sounds without consciously labelling them pleasant or unpleasant?

If you do this with others, compare notes after the walk. You might well have heard differently. However during the walk it is best to speak as little as possible. It is also interesting to record your sound walk and listen to the environmental sounds afterwards.

36.2 Cleanse your hearing.

Try wide focus hearing in as silent an environment as you can find. Put ear plugs in your ears, if necessary. Although we can never hear nothing – even in the middle of the desert there is sound energy, even with ear plugs we will hear the coursing of our own blood – this next to silence can be very cleansing.

36.3 Play with wide and narrow focus of aural attention.

Try listening more with your left, then more with your right ear. Then go back to wide focus hearing. Which is your dominant ear, that is, which ear do you habitually more frequently listen with? (You, like very many people, might actually have a difference in hearing ability between the two ears.)

Now pick out a sound and focus on it intently. Go into the aural equivalent of tunnel vision. What do you notice happens to you? Do you tense up anywhere? If so, experiment with listening without tension, that is, center yourself and keep your thoughts of lengthening and widening going. How easy is wide focus hearing when you are tense? How easy when you are centered?

Most people find they are more receptive to sound and can both listen and hear better when they are grounded and centered.

36.4 Find patterns.

Can you find patterns in the acoustic world around you? Bird song, machinery, household sounds? Can you hear patterns in your mother tongue? In a foreign language you know? Dominant sounds? Dominant pitches? Dominant rhythms? Dominant melodies?

You might like to draw these? What shapes and colours would they have?

Speaking and Habits of Listening: The Work of Alfred Tomatis

As with all narrow focus activities, we develop habits of listening just as we develop habits of doing anything else. We need to open our ears, that is, withhold consent to those habits which diminish our aural awareness, in order to speak well. We cannot make new sounds if we listen in the old ways. Hearing and speaking are part of the same neurological loop. Changes in hearing and listening bring about changes in speaking and vice versa.

This connection between hearing and speaking has been

called the "Tomatis Effect" by the French Academy of Science and Medicine, after the French doctor and audiologist Alfred Tomatis. Tomatis investigated the cause of hearing difficulties in his patients and discovered previously unknown functions of the ear and the therapeutic effects of sound. Although his work was and in some respects still is by no means unchallenged, it is gaining in recognition and his statement that the human voice can only produce what the human ear hears is accepted by many.[4] Tomatis devised a procedure of sophisticated sensory stimulation by means of electronically modified and filtered sounds listened to through a headset. Depending on the condition being treated, the individual listens to music (usually Mozart or Gregorian chants), the mother's voice, or their own voice, modified by a gating device Tomatis called the Electronic Ear. Tomatis soon found that auditory re-education often had a huge range of beneficial effects – physical and emotional – far beyond simply hearing better. Although the use of electronic equipment is not widely feasible, some of Tomatis' observations about improving listening skills can be interesting for us.

Like almost every other aspect of our lives, cultural conditioning plays a role in our habits of how we hear and listen. Our ears become attuned to those frequencies we are most used to hearing, and these include to a very large degree the dominant frequencies of the language (or languages) we grew up hearing around us. The British English ear, for example, is attuned to a much greater band of frequencies (from 2,000 – 12,000 Hertz) than the German ear (100-3000 Hertz). This does not make German speakers deaf to the higher frequencies of British English. However, it does, according to Tomatis, make them more aware of familiar frequencies and leads them to under-use those higher frequencies which lie outside their habitual hearing. This might happen when they speak English, for example, and lead to a (to British ears) monotonous way of speaking.[5] The ear can, however, gradually become attuned to different frequencies, rhythms, tones etc. If we can gradually modify the way we listen by opening our ears to the unfamiliar, we can expand our speaking skill repertoire, and not only as regards foreign languages. This might be another benefit of wide focus hearing as opposed to narrow focus listening. Anything which helps us hear non-habitually might well help us communicate more skilfully.

In addition, even if we do not hear better with one or the other, we probably have a dominant and non-dominant ear, just as most of us have a dominant and non-dominant hand, eye, and foot. We can be right-eared or left-footed, just as we can be right or left-handed. According to Tomatis, it is more beneficial for the right ear to operate as the director in those situations when we want to listen to ourselves. The right ear will receive information sooner than the left ear as no transcerebral transfer to the central laryngeal motor area (situated in the left brain) is necessary from the auditory centre of the left brain, which is where the neurological impulses from the right ear arrive. Such a transfer is however necessary from the auditory centre of the right brain, which is where the impulses from the left ear arrive.[6] In the light of this, the ability to direct listening with the right ear, investigated in exploration 36.3 might well be a useful skill.

Interestingly, for Tomatis listening involves more than just our ears. It involves the whole body and affects the whole body by mobilising the whole nervous system.[7] The ear feeds the brain with sensory stimulation, that is, energy. The function of the ear is to convert sound energy into electrical nerve impulses which the brain then sends through the entire body, toning up the whole neuromuscular system. Sound and the body are intimately connected. Here, however, it does seem to matter which frequencies the ear feeds the brain with. According to Tomatis, we need to be wary of the lower frequencies which tend to predominate. The thud, thud of the bass at very high volume in modern pop and rock music is not good brain food and can actually damage the ear. While wishing to avoid a culture debate here, it certainly makes sense to choose carefully what we listen to and which acoustic environments we put ourselves in. Some are better for us than others. Some can energise the brain, others do not.

The Mind's Ear: Inner and Outer Voices
In order to hear, listen, and speak well it can be useful to get control over our inner voices. Many of us have a verbal commentary which runs almost non-stop in our heads. Much of this is white noise or, worse, the internalised nag. Learning not to listen to this inner commentary can help us open up to the sounds which are really in the world around us. And as we stop listening to the voices inside and more to the sounds outside us, so the commentary will quieten. Going on sound walks can be useful here, and if you find yourself listening to your inner voices, just shift your attention again to the sounds outside you.

However, there is a kind of internal voice which we do want to listen to. Being able to hear in your mind's ear your own voice making sounds before you actually make them is a useful skill for everyone. This is a skill that singers, for example, hone and which for them goes by the name of pre-phonatory tuning. Mental rehearsal, even if only a split second before execution, greatly helps to prepare muscles for the real thing. A variant of this is regularly practised by sportspeople, who mentally train by seeing themselves move in their mind's eye. This effects measurable changes in muscle tone and reinforces necessary neural connections. Hearing yourself in your mind's ear is equally useful.

> **Exploration 37: Exploring your mind's ear**
> **37.1** Read a text in either your mother tongue or a foreign language silently in your head several times through. Listen to yourself in your mind's ear while remaining centered and aware of your environment.
> Do you notice any twitching or tension in your lips, tongue, jaw as if they were being used for speaking? Do you imagine the movements your tongue, lips and jaw need to make as you read?
> Then really read the text aloud, noticing how you move your tongue, lips and jaw.

Kinaesthetic Listening and Speaking

A very useful spin-off of being able to release unnecessary tension and go back to neutral is a finer and more reliable kinaesthetic awareness. Our kinaesthetic sense is often called our sixth sense. It gives us information about our position in space, movement and the relationship of the parts of our body to each other. Honing this awareness can be of benefit to those speakers who find it hard to hear and therefore produce differences between sounds. With it they can begin to orientate themselves according to how a sound feels as well as to how it sounds. The whole body is like a huge ear. This is a skill that singers and actors apply as a matter of course and is also useful for public speakers, including teachers.

Developing Your Listening Skills

Sound is movement

Sound exists as the result of something moving (vibrating) - for example the prongs of a tuning fork, the string of a guitar, the human vocal folds - which causes regions of low and high pressure immediately adjacent. These regions of oscillating molecules spread outwards in wave form; they are sound waves.[8] Sound is therefore a form of kinetic energy, that is, energy caused by things moving.

> **Exploration 38: Exploring sound as vibration**
> **38.1** Blow up a balloon and tie a knot to prevent the air from escaping. While holding the balloon lightly, bring it up to your mouth and speak and sing into it. In your hands you will feel vibration in the balloon. Experiment with different pitches and volumes and notice any difference in vibrations.

Kinaesthetic hearing

When it comes to our own speaking, we inevitably hear ourselves both externally and internally. We receive sound waves through the air with our ears and also directly through our bone and tissue. Bone conduction is faster and more immediate than conduction through air, thus we hear our own voice as louder and fuller than other people do. This is why hearing ourselves on recording devices can sometimes be quite a revelation.

This ability to hear internally, that is, kinaesthetically, as well as externally (aurally) can be trained. And it is what deaf musicians do so well by becoming very sensitive to where and how sounds they make vibrate in their body and to the precise nature of the vibration of external sounds which they can pick up. Most famously, Dame Evelyn Glennie is able to play percussion so perfectly by having trained this ability which enables her to experience sound as a form of touch. The work of Professor Paul Whittaker, who has been influential in helping deaf people access and enjoy music, is interesting in this regard.[9]

Exploration 39: Exploring kinaesthetic listening
39.1 Cover your ears with your hands or use ear plugs. Recite a text or sing a simple song. Notice the vibrations you can feel inside your head. Play around with different pitches and volumes.

39.2 Record yourself reciting the same text, once without ear plugs and then with.
What differences to your voice do you notice? How does your voice change when you cannot clearly hear the sounds you are making. Is it louder? Freer? With ear plugs were you more aware of how it feels, where the vibrations are? Were you more aware of what you were doing with your vocal apparatus?

Applications to speaking
This ability to be sensitive to internal vibration and to connect internal vibration with the use of the speaking apparatus is a highly useful skill for speakers. Its usefulness has already been implicitly touched on when we looked at the use of resonators (exploration 22). Other applications include helping speakers to distinguish between and therefore produce voiced and unvoiced consonants, and it can also be used to clarify vowels (see exploration 32).

The following exploration is better done with a partner. It is important that the person producing sound (the learner) does not primarily monitor the sound they are making but tries to focus on what they are doing and the vibrations they can sense. We are after how sound feels. The useful skill is to connect those two functions: what you do with your vocal apparatus and the vibrations you can sense. The learner needs to focus on function, not sound. It is the task of the partner (the teacher) to monitor and give feedback on the sound. If you yourself have problems hearing differences between sounds, then these explorations definitely need to be done with someone who can give you reliable feedback.

Of course, in order to produce and feel vibration well, there needs to be space for the vibrations. This means you need a lot of internal space. You need to lengthen and widen. If you shorten and narrow, then vibrations will be largely trapped and dampened. Revise chapter two, if necessary. In addition, you need to create space in your oral cavity. So dome your soft palate, allow your jaw and tongue to release. Think of lots of inner space at the back of your mouth. It is important to use your resonators, otherwise most vibration will be felt in your throat as it is not allowed to travel further. Revise chapter three, if necessary.

Exploration 40: Exploring connecting sound with kinaesthetic awareness

40.1 Experiment with the difference in vibration you can feel between unvoiced and voiced consonants. Contrast, for example: f and v (feel vs veal); p and b (pull vs bull); s and z (sing vs zing); th (unvoiced and voiced – thin vs these).

Play around with your apparatus. Try consciously to connect how you use your breath, voice and articulators with the body vibrations you feel. Remember to stay centered, with your neck, lips, tongue and jaw free.

40.2 Do exploration 32 again. For each vowel focus on tongue movement and connect your tongue movement with the sound you make as monitored by your partner. Try mirroring your different tongue shapes by making corresponding shapes with one hand.

Where do you feel any vibration? Consider all the areas of your oral cavity, forehead, nasal area, any other parts of your body.

Can you use your imagination and give each vowel sound a shape with your hands?

---

[1] See Kristin Linklater, *Freeing the Natural Voice. Imagery and Art in the Practice of Voice and Lanuage* (Nick Hern Books, London, 2006), pp.327ff, first published in the USA in 1976

[2] See Olivea Dewhurst-Maddox, T*he Book of Sound Therapy: Heal Yourself with Music and Voice* (Gaia Books, London, 1993), p.26

[3] See ibid., p.27

[4] See Alfred Tomatis, *The Conscious Ear. My Life of Transformation through Listening* (Station Hill Press, Barrytown NY, 1991), p.53, first published in French in 1977

[5] See ibid., p.72

[6] See ibid., p.51

[7] See ibid., p.206

[8] See Dewhurst-Maddox, op.cit., p.16

[9] See Music and the Deaf, www.matd.org.uk for more.

7

DEVELOPING YOUR PERFORMING SKILLS

All the world's a stage. (William Shakespeare)

As Shakespeare indicated, we are all performers. Everyday life is full of small stage entrances and exits: presenting your point of view at a meeting; telling a joke around the family dinner table; asking for something in a shop; greeting an acquaintance; making a complaint; leaving a message on voicemail, and countless other instances. For teachers there is perhaps no performance more mundane than the teaching performance, for every time we walk into a classroom we are walking on stage.

A Note on Identity
Teachers sometimes reject the notion of teaching as performing. They seem to associate it with a lack of competence and authenticity. This attitude makes them unwilling to try out anything new and encourages them to cling to habits in the name of preserving their teaching identity and sense of self. To a large degree our ways of doing are our ways of being which, in turn, are an important part of our sense of who we are. However, we need to be aware that our habits might be preventing us from being as effective teachers and communicators as we might be. Of course, not all habits deserve to be ditched. But sometimes clinging to habits in the name of "being ourselves" might be a form of self-limitation.

If identity is largely made up of habits, then we can actively construct our teaching identity by choosing our habits more consciously. As a first step, it is helpful to be open to the new, revel in experimentation, and to welcome the weird in the knowledge that if something feels weird it cannot be a habit.

Context and Culture

When choosing effective communication habits, we need, of course, to be aware that impact depends largely on context. What opens doors in one context might slam them shut in another. This can involve international differences which might well be considerable even within a relatively small territorial area. And even within the same country there will be similarities and differences between the communication cultures and subcultures of, for example, the worlds of business, academia, science, young people, to name just a few. And indeed, each educational institution will almost certainly also have its own communication culture and subcultures. The matter is complicated further by multi-cultural audiences, each member of which might well see and hear differently, and attach different meanings to elements of the performance. This context dependency and variability means that we need to be aware of context and the communication culture we are working in. In addition, it means that whatever that communication culture might be, we need to have conscious control over our own teaching performance, so that we can adapt to different audiences, situations and environments, and are not stuck in habits which may work in one context but not in another.

The Three Ingredients of Performance

Any spoken performance consists of three inseparable ingredients: the verbal (the words you speak); the physical (how you use your body and the space you find yourself in); and the vocal (your voice). All three elements are intimately connected to each other and need to be congruent in order to make a successful performance. The relative importance of each aspect varies according to situation, and of course, individual listeners will be individual in their responses. Western education tends to be logocentric; words tend to be given more value than the other elements. Unsurprisingly, many teachers then tend to focus on their words. The non-verbal factor is left largely out of account, and certainly for many teachers it appears to be frustratingly outside their conscious control.

In this chapter we take a closer look at the non-verbal elements of the teaching performance, so that we can achieve more conscious control over those vital elements and use them to better effect. The aim is to raise awareness of the potentials and possibilities which lie beyond habit.

Physical Elements of Performance

These include aspects such as:
- Posture
- Facial expression
- Use of the eyes
- Stillness and movement
- Use of space and proximity to your audience

The basis for an effective use of these which builds rapport and reinforces what you say is the self-care groundwork we looked at in chapter two. The more you are centered and aware of your own body, the more you can use it to speak for and with you. You will make a greater impact on your audience and they will be more likely to remember what you say. You will also find that being aware of the physical elements of your performance will have a big impact on your voice and will certainly influence how you think and feel and therefore what you say. Remember that the three elements of performance are inseparable.

Posture

Inevitably, we read our fellow human beings' posture, invest it with meaning, and respond to what we believe we find there.

Exploration 41: Exploring reading posture

41.1 In the light of what you have read and explored regarding centered standing (exploration 9), have a look at your fellow human beings. Look at how they stand, for example, next time you are waiting at the check-out at the supermarket or at the bus stop. Or watch a variety of TV programmes and note how people stand.

How do you respond to the variety of ways of standing you see? Do you see anyone whose way of standing attracts you? Impresses you? Why? Do you think this would be suitable in the classroom? Are there any elements you could take inspiration from and adopt or adapt for your own classroom performance? And do you see any way of standing you would rather avoid in the classroom?

41.2 Try to identify what elements of standing are communicating with you. Look, for example, at:

• alignment (is the head balancing over the torso or stuck tortoise-fashion in front?)

• balance (are both feet on the floor with weight equally

Developing Your Performing Skills

distributed, or is there a constant swaying side to side, forwards and back, weight going down only one leg, a very narrow base?)
• length (is there collapse into the pelvis, is it pushed forwards, is there collapse at the breast bone and a general sense of sagging, or a sense of lengthening and coming up to full height?)

How do you respond to what you identify?

41.3 Experiment at home with different ways of standing, using a full-length mirror. If you can imitate someone, you are probably observing well. Does a different way of standing make you feel different? Take the opportunity to practise centered standing again. Remember to find your feet. Think of your full length, connecting feet and head. Think tall and open to the world. How does it make you feel?

Facial Expression

A mobile, expressive face is an important part of communication. As already mentioned, although in the performing arts the face, and particularly the nose-eyes area, is often likened to a mask, it is in fact not a mask in the sense of being something pre-formed and rigid which we put on and take off. Neither is it something which conceals. On the contrary, your face is a highly malleable part of you which, if free, will change and respond to intention and is an integral part of yourself and your identity as a teacher. Your face will be seen and read immediately by your audience. Your facial expression can invite attention or it can push it away. Your face speaks faster and more directly than your words, so it is worthwhile getting it to work for you. Above all it needs to be alive and mobile.

Of course, our facial expression should fit what we say and

where we are. This is highly culturally conditioned and highly personal at the same time. However, although we do not want to have an empty, lips-only smile stuck to our faces all day, it is still the case that a real smile which involves the eyes is in many (although not all) teaching contexts an advantage.

Are you a smiler? Or are you parsimonious with your smiles? Do you make people work hard before you bestow a smile on them? Might you be more generous? Or more careful? How conscious are you of your smiling habits? You might like to observe yourself and those around you.

Exploration 42: Exploring your face
42.1 You have about 50 muscles in your face, so use them. Take your face to the gym and practise grimacing. Be inventive. Think of sideways, diagonal movements; toned facial muscles are a free face lift. Think also of your face as having depth. Feel it with your finger tips. The more toned and alive your facial muscles are, the more they can respond to communicative intention.

The use of your eyes

A vital part of facial expression and connection with others is the use of your eyes. In most contexts we want soft, friendly contact with the eyes, not a hard, fixed stare or avoidance of contact – unless, of course, these are the norms of the culture you are working in. It is worth remembering that we are all both givers and receivers of eye contact. The one implies the other. And it is also worth remembering that it is about making contact, not entering into a battle of wills to see who can hold the contact the longest. Ideally, we can dance a *pas de deux* with our eyes, meeting, moving away, meeting again with a different quality of contact. There is a delicacy and rhythm to the contact. Of course, how easily we deal with eye contact and how we read it does vary according to context, personality, and how we feel about the people involved, but it is useful to have skills and techniques for those occasions when we need a helping hand.

You need to give and receive eye contact in order to make rapport with your students at the beginning of each class before you say anything. And you need to include everyone, also those sitting at the sides of the room. Look right, left, in the middle. Then give the room a sweep with your gaze, from left to right and back again. This is your opportunity to get an idea of what's up with individuals and the group, to get a feel for the group on that particular day. You are gathering information as well as getting attention and creating a teacher-learner bond. If your sightlines are obstructed and if feasible, move the furniture or even better, ask your students to move it. This immediately helps to involve your students in the class, literally gets things and people moving, and makes you look confident and in control.

Coordinating eye contact with speech is another issue. The more at ease you are, the more you can improvise. However, a useful rule of thumb is one phrase per eye contact, that is, you say a phrase giving eye contact to one person, then at the next phrase give eye contact to someone else and so on. This has a natural rhythm and usually comes across as easy and personal. In most groups there is usually at least one smiler, that is, someone who habitually smiles a lot and gives eye contact. You might like to give that person eye contact first before moving on to others and the whole group.

However, be aware if you are favouring any one person or group in the class with eye contact. This will probably be noticed by the others and is open to (mis)interpretation. If there is no other reason for this predominance, notice if you are standing with your feet turned at an angle to the audience. If you are, you are probably unwittingly favouring people on the side you are turned towards. Make sure then that you are standing with your feet parallel and pointing straight in front of you.

Exploration 43: Exploring eye contact
43.1 In most contexts a soft, friendly eye contact invites people to listen and gives what you say authority. A harsh stare will turn attention away from you, and avoidance will diminish authority.
To practise softening the contact, think of looking from behind your eyes inside your skull, rather than from the surface of the eyeball.
Or focus on gaps between shapes, not on shapes themselves. For example, focus on the gaps between the leaves of a tree moving in the wind, or, when walking down a busy street, focus on the gaps between the people.
Also imagine when you walk that objects are coming towards you, rather than you towards them. Again, this is something you can practise walking down the street.

43.2 If you find giving and receiving eye contact difficult, remember to center yourself. Practise in mundane, non-threatening situations. When you walk into any room practise giving eye contact to all sides of the room. If the room is empty, imagine people are there. Then give a sweep. At home you can set up a mock class situation and recite a text coordinating phrasing and eye contact.

43.3 If all else fails, here is the tired teachers' trick:
On your listener's face draw an imaginary line just above the eyebrows and then down both cheeks to meet in a point on the chin. This is the eye triangle. If you look anywhere inside that

triangle, your listener will have the impression that you are giving them eye contact even if you may be looking straight at their nose. This is useful for those moments when you just cannot face any more faces, but be aware that the quality of contact is different from real eye contact and you probably will not feel as connected.

Stillness and Movement

This is a very important aspect we need to be aware of. We need to move in space and use gesture, but our movement and gestures need to come from a place of stillness and they need to be meaningful. Unmotivated pacing up and down, rocking from side to side, constant gesturing, playing with a pen or necklace - all of these common habits of meaningless activity, which are often crutches to distract ourselves from our nervousness, actually distract others from what we say.

The secret is to remain centered, and to realise that in this respect, as in so many others, less is more. The more we are centered, the less we need those crutches and the more we can choose when and how we move. Stillness is our home base, our default mode, so that when we do choose to move, our movement and gesture have more impact and can be used to underline what we are saying; they are not just the ever-present white noise of nervous activity which deprives all movement of meaning.

Exploration 44: Exploring meaningful movement
44.1 When you choose to gesture, then really choose and do it with conviction. Underline what you say with your hands. Precisely how you do this is largely up to you. But whatever you do, use wide, clear gestures, moving your elbows away from the sides of your body. If necessary, practise in front of a mirror. Realise that what might seem over the top to you will probably seem just right

to your audience. A lot gets lost in transmission, in the gap between you and them.

44.2 The same applies to moving through the physical space: your movement needs to be congruent with what you say, be confident, and come from a place of centered calm.

You might want spatially to mark what you say, for example, when enumerating: firstly (move to a spot in the room) – secondly (move to another place) – thirdly (move again).

Or you might want to play with proximity to your audience, moving closer and further away. Or you might want to move out of the limelight to a different part of the classroom altogether. This largely is up to you and what you want to communicate with your movement and use of space. But whatever it is, it needs to be clear and carefully chosen.

44.3 Choose a text and practise at home using gesture and movement to underline what you want to get across.

Use of Space and Proximity to your Audience

In order to use and expand our personal space we need to be aware of our physical space. We can easily develop habits which tend to shrink both us and our awareness, particularly if we feel at all nervous. We become aware only of what is immediately in front of us or lock onto certain objects or people to the exclusion of the rest of the space and people in it. We go into tunnel vision. This will make us feel (and sound) small, thin, and that we do not have or take up much space. It severely detracts from our impact. We can expand our awareness of our physical and therefore also personal space by using our peripheral vision.

Developing Your Performing Skills

Exploration 45: Exploring your physical space and peripheral vision
45.1 Look at an object at the other end of the room. Then walk towards it, keeping your eyes focused on the object and at the same time being aware of what you can see out of the corners of your eyes.
Learn to use your peripheral vision consciously both inside and outside the classroom. Your peripheral vision is about 180°.

Awareness of your physical space will help you keep and enlarge your personal space. This will add to your sense of grounded, centered calm. Being calm invites attention and will likely be perceived by others as authority.

Exploration 46: Exploring your personal space
46.1 You can practise this at home and then do it mentally in the classroom.
Center yourself. Be fully aware of your contact to the floor and your full height. Be aware of your physical space, use your peripheral vision.
Then stretch your arms out and turn around. The tips of your fingers are describing the circumference of a circle. Now imagine that circle encompassing you above, below, all around you, like a big transparent bubble. The space inside that circle is the core of your personal space. Get a sense of fully occupying that core space. Then, like the ripples on a pond after a stone has been thrown, imagine that your personal space expands in circles from that core right to the edges of the room and beyond.

This can be very useful for keeping a sense of personal space even when your physical space is small, for example, a cramped classroom or staff room, or in situations when you feel you are in too close proximity to others (pupils crowding around you, rush hour in public transport). In such situations it is particularly important that you remind yourself of your core personal space and the physical space that you do have.

Vocal Elements of Performance

These include aspects such as:
- Pitch and intonation
- Pace and pause
- Volume

Using your voice to good effect in the classroom is based, of course, on healthy self-use as outlined in the previous chapters. You will probably also notice that the aspects of physical performance touched on above have a positive impact on your voice as well. We are, after all, an integrated whole, and as we have discovered, the voice is the expression of the use of the whole self.

Pitch and Intonation

Our use of pitch and pitch variation (intonation) are part of who we believe ourselves to be and how we (want to) appear to others. Vocal pitch, that is, how high or low your voice generally tends to be, is, then, not only a matter of the length of the vocal folds (the shorter, the higher the voice). It is also a question of how you use your speaking apparatus, and, not least, the culturally encoded messages about yourself you, consciously or unconsciously, send to others.

These, of course, can change, not only as we mature, but also as social attitudes change. It is interesting to note that attitudes to the pitch of women's voices in Britain have changed since the 1950's. Just listen to old films or radio recordings and compare women's voices then and those we hear in films and radio now. On the whole, women in the public ear nowadays speak noticeably lower. It is hard to credit that this is due to a change in vocal fold length; rather it is due to a change in what women and their voices signify. For all kinds of wider cultural reasons, it appears that it has become generally desirable for women to pitch their voices lower. To speak with a high-pitched voice, which was quite the done thing in the 1950's, is now regarded as "little girly" and lacking in authority.

Intonation is an essential part of all languages and each has its own dominant pitch patterns. And in tonal languages, of course, meaning is given by pitch variation. But even in non-tonal languages such as English, intonation can be used to convey subtleties of meaning, attitude, and identity. For many listeners, your use of intonation is an indicator of how you really feel about your audience and what you are saying, with all the possibilities of misunderstanding that entails, particularly for foreign speakers and listeners. However, in many cases, we use intonation habitually and are quite unaware of how we are using our voices and the possibilities and potentials we might have.

The following explorations are intended to raise your awareness of your vocal possibilities, so that you can be more flexible depending on language and context. How you then decide to use your instrument is up to you, which language you are speaking, and what you want to convey.

Exploration 47: Exploring pitch
47.1 Imagine your voice is a lift which smoothly glides up and down a department store.
On the vowel sound "oo" let the lift run from the basement to the

top floor and down again, i.e. from the bottom of your range to the top. Remember that the store does not move as the lift moves. Allow your voice to move up and down while keeping your shoulders, head, eyes, eyebrows and jaw calm. Keep your larynx released, throat open and neck free.

Feel how the vibrations move up and down inside you from your chest to ideally the top of your skull as the pitch moves. Try to travel as smoothly as possible, avoiding any bumps or gaps, especially when going down. Slow down at those points. Above all, keep the air flowing.

This can also usefully be done lying down in the active resting position.

47.2 When that is going well, every now and then the lift stops on a floor and you can announce that floor using the relevant pitch: For example, Basement – furniture; Ground floor – cosmetics; first floor – ladies' fashions; second floor – children's wear; top floor – restaurant. Use your lowest pitch for basement and highest for top floor. Remember to slide between announcing each floor.

You can also underline the movement of the lift by raising and lowering one arm as your voice rises and lowers in pitch.

Consciously notice the range of your voice and the vibrations in your body, where they are, and how they feel.

47.3 If you would like to make your general pitch lower, then bring in more of the basement and ground floor vibrations. If you would like to make it higher, then bring in more of the top floor vibrations. Remember that you can slide smoothly in the lift. Ideally we are aiming for a mixed voice, one which mixes the resonances and vibrations from all floors of the department store. This is your unique, integrated voice.[1]

47.4 Monitor where you tend to pitch your speaking voice in everyday life. Is it context-dependent? Does your voice tend to get higher in pitch in certain situations, e.g. if you are anxious, or when talking to certain people (children, perhaps)? If you can speak more than one language, do you tend to have a different general pitch depending which language you are speaking? Just notice what your habits are and be aware that you could change them if you would like.

47.5 Sing! Sing as much and as often as you can: in the shower (bathrooms usually have flattering acoustics), in the car, doing the washing-up. Sing along to the radio, your personal stereo, or a CD. It is unimportant whether you can hold a tune or not, the main thing is to get pitch variation and just to enjoy using your voice.

47.6 Try singing instead of speaking. This is real fun to do with friends.
Sing a conversation. Or if you are alone, sing the thoughts you would think silently to yourself.
You can play around with your own melodies, make your own opera. Experiment with more florid aria-type sentences with a big range. Play around with more simple, folksong-like melodies with a small range.
You might well find that you also start to use some aspects of physical performance without thinking about them: you might use gesture, space, facial expression. If you find yourself doing this, go with it.
Then speak but imagine you are singing. If you are doing this with friends, give each other feedback. Listen to and watch your friends.

Pace and Pause

How fast or slow we speak and how we use pauses are essential elements of every spoken performance. By using pace and pause skilfully, we can add a huge amount to what we say and attract and hold our audience's attention. And of course, by adding pauses, we make life easier both for ourselves and for our audience; we all need pauses in order to keep track of what we are saying and in order to digest what has been said. As so often, speaker and listener have similar needs.

Exploration 48: Exploring pace and pause
48.1 In days of yore (and perhaps sometimes still today), monks used to chant and pray aloud while quite literally pacing. This gives the chanting a steady rhythm as speech and movement merge and influence each other.

You can try this out with the Latin text below. I've chosen Latin in order to slow you down and to encourage you to focus on sound rather than meaning. Do not worry about correct pronunciation or understanding of the text. Just relish the sounds you make and think of communicating that relish.

Slowly walk in as large a circle as space will permit. When you feel you have established a slow, calming, regular pacing rhythm, recite the first line, keeping that regular pacing rhythm. At the end of the line, keep pacing and pause in your recitation for two paces. Then recite the second line and so on. Keep the regular pacing rhythm going throughout, making sure you do not speed up.

When this is going well, you can vary the exploration by first clearly establishing the regular pacing rhythm before each line and then stopping to recite each line.

It is important that you still feel and keep to the pacing rhythm as you speak.

Here is the text:
Adiutur laborantium
Bonorum rector omnium
Custos ad propugnaculum
Defensorque credentium,
Exaltator humilium
Fractor superbentium

Developing Your Performing Skills

Gubernator fidelium
Hostis inpoenitentium ...

48.2 Play with pace and pause.
Recite any simple text. Children's nursery rhymes are often useful here. First mark in where you are going to pause, at places which make sense, and decide how long or short, as in the example below:

Oh, the grand old duke of York, (short)
He had ten thousand men, (longer)
He marched them up to the top of the hill, (no pause)
And he marched them down again. (long)
And when they were up, they were up, (short)
And when they were down they were down, (short)
And when they were only half way up, (long, for suspense)
They were neither up nor down. (long)

Start slowly and then gradually speed up. Make sure you are maintaining clear articulation. And make sure you are keeping the pauses clear and the long pauses long, however fast you speak.
Speeding up means you move your tongue and lips faster, it does not mean that you shorten or cut out the pauses. The number and length of the pauses should not change as your speaking pace changes.
Then slow down once more, again keeping the long pauses long and the short ones short.

Volume

Volume, that is, how loudly or softly you speak, can be an element of performance if used consciously and with skill. You do not want to push and shout to increase volume, nor do you want to collapse and let your voice get trapped in your throat to reduce volume. Your body needs to function well to speak both loudly and softly. Re-read and re-explore chapter three, if necessary.

Exploration 49: Exploring volume
49.1 Make a sound bath. This exploration is ideal in a group.
Make a close circle, everyone facing inwards. Everyone then turns 180° so that all are facing outwards, but still in a circle and close together. Each member then makes up their own melody (most people will automatically harmonise) on any sequence of vowel sounds, thinking of sending the sound through their back into the centre of the circle behind them. Each can also receive the sound through their back, aware of how sound is swirling in the circle behind them.
When there is a good solid group sound going, turn 180° again so that all are facing inwards. The signal to turn can be pre-arranged as the responsibility of one member, or it can be done intuitively by the group (this really does work, provided this has been flagged up at the beginning).

49.2 When there is a good group sound going, members of the group can take it in turns to go into the centre of the circle and bathe in the sound.
Each member of the group can play with increasing and decreasing volume. Most people will automatically be sensitive to differences in volume. In this way each member can contribute to making a harmonious group sound as well as experimenting with their individual sound making.

49.3 If you are on your own, you can do this exploration.
Choose an object in the room. Put yourself at a distance to it, turn your back to it and speak, chant or hum to it. When you have established a firm sound, turn around to face the object and continue to vocalise, still keeping the idea of sending sound out through your back.
You can then increase and decrease your distance from the

object and play with different volumes. You can also play with turning your back to it and then turning to face it as in a dance.

Notice if you unintentionally reduce volume when facing the object. Try to speak facing the object while maintaining volume. Be very careful you do not poke your head forwards when you want to increase volume. Maintain the thought of speaking also through your back.

49.4 You can also do this exploration on your own.

Stand at one end of the room, and go into bowling position, putting one foot in front of the other. With the opposite arm to whichever foot is in front, throw imaginary tennis balls to the far corners, using an underarm throw. As you let the ball fly, say a number. Let your voice and eyes follow the imaginary ball as it makes an arc up and over to the other side of the room.

Make sure your back stays back and your head stays over your torso (no poking forwards). Really think of your voice copying the ball's trajectory to reach the corner of the room.

Increasing Your Skill in Using Intonation, Pace and Volume

Very frequently we combine the three elements of intonation, pace, and volume. For example, when we speak with a higher pitch we also often speak faster. In this exploration we are playing with isolating each element so that we can use each one with more skill and awareness.

Exploration 50: Exploring separating intonation, pace, and volume

50.1 This is a partner exploration.

A holds the remote control of a TV set; B is the TV which will be controlled remotely by A. Together they agree on non-verbal body signals to indicate:

- get louder /get softer

Harriet Anderson: The Thinking Teacher's Body

- get faster / get slower
- more pitch variation / less pitch variation

For example: to indicate "get louder" A could spread their arms out to the sides, to indicate "get softer" A could bring their hands together. The precise signals are not important; what matters is that they are simple to carry out, both A and B understand them, and that they do not involve speaking.

B counts out loud (this simply so that B does not have to think about what to say). A will use the agreed signals to indicate change in volume, pace, and intonation. A must gesture clearly and also give B time to make the changes.

A needs to be listening for whether the changes requested are really carried out clearly, and also whether only the change requested is carried out and not a change in another aspect as well. Give each other feedback.

Swap roles.

Verbal Elements of Performance

To deal in any depth with the verbal elements of the teaching performance, that is, what you say, would stray into territory which goes far beyond the remit of this book. However, it is worth being aware that the verbal and non-verbal performances are co-dependent. Our fluency and ability to find the right word while speaking are influenced by our bodily state. If we freeze physically, we will also freeze mentally and verbally. While speaking, it is therefore important to stay centered and with the potential for movement.

Of course, when used in conjunction with the appropriate words, the physical and vocal elements outlined above act as impact strategies which attract and keep your audience's attention. You can, for example, use variation in volume, pace, and pause, to underline the main ideas you want to get across.

Developing Your Performing Skills

In addition, you can speak to your listener's body by choosing language which appeals to the senses, including the kinaesthetic sense. Doing this will help to balance any intellectual overload. Metaphors, images and stories also appeal to the senses as well as to the intellect and the emotions. These can be helpful not only to make what you say more memorable, but also to make abstract ideas concrete and more easily understandable. In general, the more your words can speak to body, mind and emotions, the better.

Speaking with the Whole Self

Our goal is the congruence of the physical, vocal and verbal elements to make an integrated performance, where all three elements enhance each other. If we can manage that, we can establish the necessary three-way connection: to ourselves, to what we are saying, and to our audience. We can then speak with authenticity and engagement.

When practising the physical and vocal elements at home, it can be useful to exaggerate. Remember that something always gets lost in the gap between you and your audience. You can always tone things down if necessary. But it is hard to ratchet things up if you have not learnt to feel comfortable with, for example, making big gestures and having a big voice when in a protected situation such as at home. So start big, and then reduce if you need to.

It is important that this process of toning down is a choice and not a habit. You need to be consciously modifying your performance, not because you are staying within your comfort zone, or because you just cannot use your body and voice in any other way, but because you choose to do so. This is the deeper goal we are after: that we are choosing the elements of our teaching performance, because we have acquired skill and freed ourselves from confining habits.

Exploration 51: Exploring speaking with the whole self
51.1 Play around with different moods.
Say a sentence, for example, "Hello, my name is (add your own name)" in various moods, including any gestures, facial expression, use of space you think appropriate for that mood. Use the whole range of your voice; really get the intonation of that mood clear. Possible moods might be: surprised; tired; angry; happy; sad; puzzled; bored …

51.2 Chuck out the garbage with gusto.
Imagine the space in front of you is a garbage bin. Throw your garbage into the bin, making the appropriate noises of disgust and the facial grimaces and gestures to go with it. Do it with gusto.

51.3 Combine with text.
Recite poetry, sing songs and read young children's storybooks aloud. Really enter into the meaning. Consider also how you would like your audience to feel. Imagine you are telling a story to a group of alert five-year-olds who are slightly hard of hearing. Use lots of variation in volume, pace, pitch. Use facial expression, gesture. Use your space. Exaggerate.

When you speak, get used to making more of your body and voice and their huge potential for expression.

Daily Practice and Warm-up Routine
This ties in with the content of chapters two and three and builds on the daily voice care routine outlined in chapter three. You can do the routine outlined there and add the following elements:

Developing Your Performing Skills

- Facial grimaces – take your face to the gym
- Hum, thinking also of the sound coming out of your back. Hum softer and then louder
- Slides up and down your range
- The Grand Old Duke of York at different speeds, paying attention to keeping pauses and clear articulation; use intonation to fit the "ups" and "downs" of the story
- Play around with moods
- Chuck out the garbage with gusto

Troubleshooting

When dealing with all these common problems, remember to center yourself first.

Speaking too fast:
- Listen to yourself while you speak; this will almost certainly slow you down and make you pay more attention to how you use yourself.
- Think in chunks of meaningful language, not individual words, and put in pauses after each chunk.
- Monitor your audience reactions; these are often a good indicator of whether you are speaking too fast.
- Remember that less is more: speaking more slowly and perhaps therefore saying less in an allotted time so that your audience can follow you, is of more value than cramming a lot of speech into the time but at such a speed that your audience shuts down or has to struggle to keep up. If you have little time, re-think your content; do not speed up your delivery.

Monotonous speaking voice:
- raise your soft palate
- sing what you would say, then think of singing as you speak
- lift exploration (exploration 47.1)
- moods (exploration 51.1)

Coordinating breathing with speaking:
- Allow your breath out, then it will come in
- Think and speak in chunks of meaning not individual words
- Consciously breathe out at the end of each meaningful chunk

Overly nasal or pinched voice:
- Use your resonators more
- Remember to activate your soft palate and keep your tongue released
- Think of allowing your voice to inhabit the whole of your body and your space. Allow it to spread.

Flapping hands:
- Stop and center yourself, consciously speak without any gestures and get used to stillness, even if it feels very weird and "wrong". Practise in front of a large mirror.
- Add large gestures, exaggerate, then tone down
- Practise stillness in everyday life
- Notice your everyday use of gesture. Cut out those which you notice are habits. Allow your gestures to come from a place of calm

Habitual pacing:
- Stop and center yourself
- Get used to speaking and standing without movement
- Then add centered movement, letting it come from a place of calm. Remember your centered standing.
- Plan movement and gesture in conjunction with text. Preparation is the key to spontaneity. The more secure we feel with a rehearsed performance, the more we can then deviate from our plan and allow ourselves to be inspired.

---

[1] See Kristin Linklater, *Freeing the Natural Voice. Imagery and Art in the Practice of Voice and Language* (Nick Hern Books, London, 2006), pp.275-8, first published in USA in 1976

PART THREE

FIRST PRINCIPLES RE-VISITED

The more experiments you make, the better.
(Ralph Waldo Emerson)

8

WIDER CLASSROOM APPLICATIONS

I am always doing that which I cannot do, in order that I may learn how to do it. (Pablo Picasso)

So far we have considered how you can promote your own well-being in the classroom and also how you can hone your speaking, listening and performing skills. Yet can the first principles, which have inspired our explorations so far, also have wider classroom relevance? How could they be applied to aspects such as lesson planning and assessment, for example? And could they go even further and enrich the human side of teaching and learning by promoting qualities such as creativity and a supportive atmosphere in the classroom?

My thoughts on possible wider classroom applications of our first principles are mainly coloured by my own experiences in the world of foreign language teaching and learning and from working with many foreign language teachers. I draw my examples from that world. However, teaching languages is by no means unique and I am sure that teachers of other subjects, particularly those which have a skills component, will find many parallels to their own experiences.

The Value of Challenging Habits

The ability to stop and withhold consent to habitual responses, which we have frequently explored in previous chapters, is the lynchpin of all change. Its benefits go far beyond the aspects we have already explored. It can be beneficially applied anywhere habit rules and constrains. Like all arenas of human interaction, classrooms tend to be places where habits dominate. And like all human beings, teachers tend to be creatures of habit. Most teachers, early in their careers, develop habits of teaching or simply accept established teaching practice for their subject. These habits often stay with them for years, unquestioned and unexplored. Some of those habits will be beneficial, but others will not. The ability to stop and withhold consent to habit helps us to escape its limiting power over us. Essentially, by doing so, we can open the door to innovation and the potential for new forms of teaching and learning. We can reflect more on our own teaching practice and so become more skilful teachers. Challenging habits can stretch from considering our choices about what kind of teacher-learner relationship we want and how we set boundaries, to the nitty gritty of lesson preparation and course content.

Take lesson planning, for example. One of the most frequent, unquestioned lesson planning habits I have come across whenever some aspect of skill acquisition is involved, is the idea that you "do" theory first and then go on to the practice. Theory and practice are seen as two distinct and separate entities. And they are explicitly presented as such to the learner, whereby the theory part often means a lot of teacher talking time and passive learners. The theory/practice divide becomes also a passive/active divide. So, for example, foreign language learners will first have new grammatical structures and rules explained to them and only then move onto identifying those structures in a text and lastly actively use them themselves. Of course, the helpfulness of the theory/

practice divide will to some extent depend on the subject matter. Yet in very many cases, creating a sharp division makes it more difficult for the learner to acquire both the theory and the practice. Cognitive understanding emerges from doing, just as doing is illuminated by cognitive understanding. They are inseparable, two sides of the same coin. Yet too frequently it is left to the learner to re-unite what the teacher has sundered. Instead of following this divisive "theory, then practice" model, teachers could instead use a more fluid one. They could use carefully chosen practice to merge into theory and then let theory merge into practice. So, for example, foreign language learners themselves could deduce and attempt a first formulation of new grammatical structures and rules from carefully chosen texts (written and spoken), go on to use them, and then using teacher feedback and further text input proceed to refine and re-formulate the rules. Yet whatever teachers decide to do, the main point is that they have decided and are not merely following habit.

Another, connected, lesson planning habit which could be challenged would be the idea that the methodological ideal is an activity-packed lesson, where students move seamlessly from one activity or task to another. This certainly seems to be a dominant ideal in the language teaching world. It is implicit in a huge number of teacher resource books along the lines of "what you can do with your pupils", with often very imaginative ideas for graded activities and lists of needed materials which would sometimes put a handicraft shop to shame. Yet despite the coloured cards, felt-tip pens, laminated posters and other accoutrements, does student activity necessarily and always promote learning? Obviously not, if that activity is done without understanding. And it is certainly my experience that activity needs to be tempered by stopping and reflecting. Both teacher and students need the time to reflect in order to become aware of what they have learned through an activity and to verbalise that awareness either privately for themselves or publicly in class.

We need to place a greater value on exploring stopping within activity. This is true for all age groups. In the context of lesson planning this could mean allocating quiet time or time for self-directed study within a lesson. Many students can direct their own learning if given the well set-up opportunity. It might mean allocating reflection time in class and encouraging students to verbalise what they have learnt either in writing or speech. Learning logs can here be useful if used sensibly. And sometimes, quite simply, silence is golden.

Exploring stopping and withholding consent to habit in the classroom also means giving yourself and your students time: time to think, time to formulate questions, time to answer, time to understand. This can mean adjusting your, and their, expectations and even values. It can mean permitting yourself and your students to put in a pause between question and answer, rather than obeying the expectation of an immediate response. It can mean permitting yourself and your students to say "I don't know" and to find out later. It can mean devising ways of valuing process just as much as (if not more than) the finished product. Guided re-writes could, for example, be made an integral part of the learning process, rather than a form of correction.

Giving time and valuing process can also mean giving repetition a higher value than might often be the case. Repetition seems to have a bad press. Frequently it is seen as boring (been there, done that), or evidence of failure (too stupid, lazy, inattentive to learn first time round). But repetition has an important part to play in learning. The brain needs repetition for new neural pathways to be established, and the body needs even more repetition to feel comfortable with the new and turn it into the familiar. And re-visiting the familiar while learning the new can also promote a sense of achievement and therefore boost enjoyment, self-confidence, and motivation.

> **Exploration 52: Exploring challenging habits**
> **52.1** The flipped classroom model.
> First, assign what you would normally cover in the lesson as homework. Then do what is usually considered homework in class time with everyone.
> Let us take an example from standard foreign language teaching: the teaching of a new tense. Instead of introducing in class how the new tense is formed (as is normally done), the teacher could ask the students to read the relevant pages in the course book for homework. Then in class the students could do and discuss the tense practice exercises, which in standard pedagogy are often set as homework.
> This flipped classroom model shakes up student and teacher expectations and roles. For instance, that it is the role of the teacher to present the theory and the role of the student to put it into practice. It also encourages self-directed learning as the pupils can stop at any time, repeat, take notes in their own time etc.

The Usefulness of Mistakes

Mistakes are learning opportunities. This might be a truism, but all too often it is one which is forgotten in teaching and learning practice. Frequently, the fear of making a mistake and attendant loss of face, even when it is masked by an apparent insouciance, is one of the biggest obstacles to learning. Anything which helps the student and also the teacher feel that they do not have to be right, promotes teaching and learning. Learning in its essence is about what we cannot yet do or do not yet know. Mistakes are, then, merely evidence of our "not yet" state. This is, for example, recognised in language pedagogy, where errors are regarded as a natural part of language learning.[1] Every learner (including children learning their mother tongue) must pass through an interlanguage, that is, a learner language which gradually evolves as the learner receives more input and their knowledge of the target language increases. There is no other way of learning language than through making mistakes. And probably that goes for all learning.

Yet all too often, mistakes are seen as something bad. Students generally learn very early on in their educational careers that mistakes are to be avoided and that that avoidance will be rewarded by better grades. Altogether the focus for both teacher and student is often not on how much a student got right, but on how much they got wrong. This takes the form of identifying mistakes with apparent ease (there is often no discussion about what qualifies as a mistake and why), counting them, even categorising them into "big" and "small" mistakes, and above all bringing them to the student's attention by means of red ink and verbal admonishment. Students thereby learn caution and the fear of experimentation. They learn to stay with the known, with what they feel sure about, and they learn that experimentation is risky and might be penalised. An unhelpful, self-limiting habit has been learnt. Above all, this is a habit which undermines creativity, learning and liveliness in the classroom. Qualities such as these are rooted in self-confidence and in curiosity. They cannot flourish in an atmosphere where being right is given precedence.

These common attitudes to mistakes are, of course, reflections of what is prevalent in society outside the classroom. Education values are embedded in a wider social context and usually reinforce the dominant values of society as a whole. Although we as teachers probably cannot hope to change the wider context of values in which we work and live, we can in a small way challenge these attitudes.

Firstly, in student evaluations (which often take the form of giving grades) we can shift the emphasis from debit to credit. We can give marks rather than take them away. We can focus on the positive, on what has been learnt, rather than on the negative, on what has (not yet) been learnt.

Secondly, we can welcome mistakes as learning opportunities and use them as such. Mistakes can open doors. We can see mistakes as sources of information and feedback for ourselves. They show us the current understanding of the student and whether anything needs to be dealt with again or in a different manner. Mistakes carry information and it is our task to interpret that information and take it seriously.

Thirdly, we can develop in ourselves and perhaps also in our students a more forgiving attitude to being wrong and a more questioning attitude to being right. It can be liberating for both teacher and students to shed the burden of the need to be right, and all the baggage attached to that: status, authority, self-esteem. Being right so easily merges into being in the right, that is, being right acquires a moral dimension, it becomes an attribute of personal value. To realise on a deep level that personal value is not dependent on being right but exists independent of it can be immensely liberating. In turn, that liberation makes for a less fearful and therefore a more lively, creative and productive classroom.

And finally, challenging these prevalent attitudes to mistakes also leads to a consideration of how mistakes are defined. What is a mistake? What is an error? How do they differ? According to what criteria or authority do we judge? Do rightness and wrongness in fact lie on a continuum rather than inhabiting two different universes? Are correct/right and incorrect/wrong context dependent? In some cases, these questions might be discussed in class with concrete examples taken from the matter in hand (language learning is full of such cases), in other cases it might be more profitable for the teacher to ponder them alone.

Exploration 53: Exploring your attitudes to mistakes
53.1 What would you say are your general attitudes to mistakes (as defined by you), both inside and outside the classroom. On the whole are you more tolerant of mistakes made by others than by yourself, or not? Are your attitudes context dependent? For example, is there a difference in your attitudes to mistakes made in a professional context to those made in a private context?

53.2 Take a step backwards and become your own coach. Is there anything about your attitudes to mistakes that you would like to change? Can you transfer from one context of your life where you feel content with your attitudes to mistakes and apply to another where you are not so content? (Re-read exploration 27.)

53.3 How do you tend to deal with learner mistakes in the classroom? Consider a mistake frequently made by your pupils. What repertoire of responses do you have at your finger tips?

In a foreign language teaching situation, for example, possible responses to a mistake include: ignoring it; supplying the correct version (re-casting) and passing on; explicitly correcting; reprimanding; asking the rest of the class to correct; making a note of mistakes and correcting at the end of the class; having a special class on frequent mistakes; asking the class to revise that topic; asking the pupil making the mistake to try again, revise, do extra work, do an extra test. Do you have any non-verbal signals (tone of voice, gesture, facial expression) which indicate to your students when you are correcting? How do you make certain that your correction (e.g. a re-cast) is understood as such?

Consider that you have a repertoire of responses, all of which might be effective. Which one you choose to employ when is dependent on your focus in that lesson and what you want to achieve. Responding to mistakes and making constructive use of them is a skill. And the basis of that skill is stopping your habitual responses and giving yourself the time to choose how you want to respond.

A Note on Concentration

Like making mistakes, learner concentration (or the lack of it) is a topic surrounded by many assumptions and habits of thought in the educational world. In standard classroom pedagogy, narrow focus attention, usually going by the label "concentration", is regarded as highly desirable and the precondition to learning. Uncontrolled sensory input is unwelcome, indeed regarded as a distraction, and banished from the classroom as far as possible. The ideal is that the learner should diminish the range of their attention, usually to the size of an A4 piece of paper. Invariably, this sensory shrinking is accompanied by a physical shrinking and a lot of muscle tension: the student twists their feet around chair legs, tightens their neck and jaw, their eyes stare or glaze over, they frown, tighten their tongue or even stick it out, hold their breath, and generally slump over the desk, gripping any book or writing implement with tense fingers. This is the picture of "concentration" welcomed in many classrooms and regarded by many teachers as proof of learning.

Concentration of this kind is, however, really a form of closing down. Mind and body become smaller, narrower, and shut off from the world around. Far from being favourable to learning, concentration of this kind is actually more of an obstacle. The ideal state for receiving and processing new input, which is what learning is about, is a unified field of awareness: a calm, alert, and open mind, and a centered, lengthening and widening body which is using only the necessary amount of muscle tension for the task in hand. The unified field of awareness which we have incorporated into many explorations earlier in this book, enables us to be agile in our attention; we can move from sensory input to intellectual activity and back again with ease. That is, we can choose where we place our attention, without losing contact with the outside world and our sensory awareness of it. Like a camera zoom lens, we can adjust focus at will. And we can choose not to let our attention get snagged by distractions, that is, by those stimuli which do not promote our learning or teaching.

The mind-wandering much dreaded by teachers is actually a product of the loss of the unified field of awareness. Paradoxically, this is caused by the effort to concentrate and its physical manifestations. The effort to concentrate is, then, a precondition of loss of attention. Distraction occurs when we do not have the necessary agility in attention. We are clumsy as regards awareness and attention; we are unskilled in our use of the zoom lens. In the case of both what is usually regarded as concentration and distraction, it is often helpful to center ourselves, to come back to our body and our immediate sensory input. This means sending our awareness to our contact with support (the floor, the chair), to our breathing, to the sensations of our skin (temperature, touch, clothing), to our awareness of light and shade. Then, when we are both calmer and more alert, we can come back to the task in hand while still maintaining our awareness. In addition, by opening up our sensory awareness, we will be more receptive to multi-sensory learning.

Exploration 54: Exploring your unified field of awareness

54.1 The next time you are engaged in a desk-based task which demands concentration, experiment with the following tactics. After each tactic return to the task in hand, while maintaining awareness of the sensory input you have just received:

Shift your gaze to the ceiling, then back again
Walk to other side of room, then back again
Look out of the window on purpose, in a mental gesture of getting outside the room
Promote your body awareness: awareness of how you are sitting, breathing, areas of tension (jaw etc), use your peripheral vision
Do some of the voice explorations
Do some of the hearing and listening explorations

54.2 Do the same exploration with your students. Choose one tactic per session and after each tactic let your students come back to the task at hand.
These are the tactics which everyone else has been trying to stop your pupils doing in the effort to make them "concentrate".

Become a guerrilla.

"What?" versus "How?"

One of our most pervasive and harmful habits is that of focusing exclusively on achieving what we want (end gaining), rather than giving equal if not more consideration to how we achieve what we want (attending to means as well as ends). Yet withholding consent to that habit of end gaining might be very useful in a wide range of teaching situations and is almost always a consideration when we set our students tasks. Are we only after the "what", that is, task fulfilment? Or are we also concerned with the "how", for frequently the two do not go hand in hand? The former (the what) often becomes a form of end gaining. It is informed by the spirit of closure. The goal is to complete the task or whatever else is demanded, sometimes as quickly as possible and usually with as few mistakes as possible. But it might well be done mindlessly, following rote patterns, and with no real understanding or ability to apply those patterns in other contexts. The "what" has triumphed. The "how", on the contrary, is informed more by a spirit of curiosity and is open to what we might discover on our way to our goal. It is done with awareness and is the path to learning. The "what" is driven by narrow focus attention; the "how" by wide focus awareness.

If we consider means as well as ends then we, as teachers, will not be content with right answers alone. Take students doing a "fill in the gaps" exercise, still ubiquitous in language teaching. Merely saying "yes" to a right answer and then moving on to the next one closes a door and shuts down the mind. In fact, it prevents students from going as far as they might, and reinforces the belief that being right is the essence of learning. Attending to the means, that is, asking leading questions about how students arrived at the right answer will, on the contrary, open new doors through which they can progress. One could ask the students why they have given the answer they have. What knowledge, skills and understanding have they called upon to come to this decision? Often students are not aware of how they reach an answer, or they might just reach the right answer through luck.

To make students more aware of this process of decision making, they can, for example, be divided into small groups. One member is assigned the role of taking the minutes of the decision making process. The minutes are then discussed in class. Asking "How did you arrive at your answer?" and not only (or even) "What is the right answer?" invites students to become more aware and gain a deeper understanding of the subject matter. They can also be asked to consider other answers, even if they are not correct. Students can learn a lot by exploring why wrong answers are wrong. And they might discover that there is often not only one right answer but several, or even different ways of being right. In my experience, this is particularly helpful in language teaching and can radically alter students' approach to language. For many students the realisation that there can be different ways of being right is a revelation and often a challenge, because it forces them out of the dominant right/wrong scheme of binary thinking. This scheme of thinking, however reassuring, gives learners a false sense of security and might often be actually misleading. And asking students to consider the "how" as well as the "what" is beneficial not only for advanced students; it is just as helpful for beginners as well. All students can profit from increased awareness.

Wider Classroom Applications

The same, of course, is true of teachers. End-gaining attitudes are increasingly taking over mainstream education. It is becoming more and more crudely target-driven, making life hard for teachers who want to take a different approach and work according to a different set of values. Yet even if we reject target-driven education, how far do we nevertheless orientate ourselves to achieving results according to pre-conceived ideas of what those results should be and neglectful of the perhaps many and varied ways of achieving those results? And how open are we to other results than those we envisage? In a classroom context following a more "how" attitude which values means as well as ends, might include things like: attending to your own and your students' well-being in the classroom; abandoning a lesson plan when you see it is not working well and taking a more open and improvisational approach; allowing yourself and your students more time; perceiving mistakes as a learning opportunity for yourself and your students, to name just a few.

Exploration 55: Exploring attending to the "how"
55.1 How often do you find yourself doing tasks which you "just want to get done and out of the way", but find you neglect to consider the means whereby, that is, how you fulfil those tasks?
For example, attending to the "how" when using a computer might mean observing how you sit and asking yourself whether you could sit with more ease. This will probably include being aware of your contact to support under your feet and sitting bones, thinking of your lengthening spine, and allowing your breath to flow. And it means keeping these thoughts going while you write.
This might sound like a lot of extra work and effort, but in fact you will almost certainly find that the task becomes more pleasurable and interesting as a result. By attending to process we give

ourselves and what we do value and dignity, however boring or irritating the task in hand might be.

55.2 Experiment with stopping what you are doing as soon as you notice that the attitude of "just getting the job done" becomes dominant. Develop sensitivity to that tipping point when you start to end gain. Get up and walk away. Do something else. Then come back to your task. Or not. It is your choice.

Excursus: Stray Thoughts on Fear, Fun and Learning
Contained in this more reflected attitude to how we achieve our goals is perhaps a new thoughtfulness about the role of fear in the learning process.[2] My guess is that almost everyone has experienced fear in some form while trying to learn something. This need not necessarily be academic learning in a formal context such as in school. It can also apply to learning in other contexts and cover a whole range of non-academic skills, such as any kind of performing in front of an audience (which many people find truly terrifying), driving a car (ditto), assertiveness in conflict situations (ditto) – or anything else.

It seems to me that the most common approach to teaching someone to do something which causes them fear is, fundamentally, to push the learner to do it anyway. It is the "just do it" school of thinking and teaching, even if it is usually not made so explicit. The learner might be coaxed instead of bullied or cajoled, but fundamentally the focus is still on goal achievement. It seems to me, however, that this is a form of end-gaining, of putting the "what" before the "how". My own experience of fear and learning is that this method might well lead to results, but these results are external and limited. The external goal (driving the car from A to B, performing on stage, holding a speech) has been achieved. But it has still been achieved with fear. There has been no real change in the emotional content. So, for example, the business man who is afraid of giving presentations (and there are many in this position) might well be able to force himself to give presentations and learn to give them with reasonable success, but will still experience fear. The change has occurred on the outside, not the inside. But it is changing the business man's subjective experience of giving a presentation which will really make a difference to his quality of life and is the more profound change.

In standard pedagogy, it seems to me that "fun" is often presented as a solution to fear and a lubricant to learning. In practice this seems to mean using humorous cartoons, playing games, showing comic videos, or generally adopting a jocular tone and manner. "Infotainment" rules. Although I don't doubt the value of taking a more light-hearted approach in some teaching situations, my experience as both a learner and teacher has been that "fun" of this kind does not really address issues of fear and does not present a real alternative to the "just do it" school of teaching, learning and thinking. On the contrary, it acts as a mask. In addition, this kind of "fun" too often misses its target and feels weary and pre-packaged. Having "fun" becomes yet another teacher expectation to be met by the learner.

So what alternatives do we have? Well, following our first principles, if we shift our focus from the "what", the end goal, to the "how", to how we achieve that end goal, then perhaps we can get a handle on fear. We looked at psycho-physical aspects of this in chapter four, above all the immensely beneficial power of pausing and centering.

Building on the insights of chapter four, we can also shift the focus to the "how" by re-framing fear as a by-product of learning, rather than seeing it as evidence of personal weakness or inadequacy, as is often the case. This re-framing can take many forms. For many learners, for example, fear is connected to having learnt the habit of connecting self-worth to success. The prospect of lack of success (even if only temporary), which is unavoidable and integral to the learning process, then becomes terrifying as so much rides on it. In other cases, for example learning to drive a car, fear might well be a sign of an intelligent learner who is aware of what they do not (yet) know and cannot (yet) do and has a protective function. It is simply a by-product of learner awareness. In another case, for example fear of entering a room full of strangers at a party, we could perceive that fear as a product of not having learnt when we were younger a few of the basic survival skills of how to deal with such a situation. But in all cases, if we can re-think fear and turn it from being a sign of personal inadequacy to being merely something which is connected to an unfinished or unhelpful learning process (either what we have learnt, or did not learn, in the past or a by-product of learning in the present), we can open a door to change. Fear becomes less personal.

Another aspect of teaching which shifts the focus to the "how" is to allow the pupil to go at their own pace and trust in the transformative powers of learning, rather than seeing the teacher as leading or even dragging the pupil towards goal achievement. Letting the pupil lead means seeing the teacher as one who walks beside the pupil, offering a supporting hand when needed, but fundamentally allowing the learner to determine the pace and direction of their learning. This is particularly important if issues of fear are involved. In practice this means allowing the pupil to take a succession of little steps and to repeat and consolidate each one until they are really ready to take the next small step. This might include the teacher suggesting what the next small step could be. But it is the teacher's job to listen to the pupil, be patient and to show trust in the pupil's capacity to learn. Learning, that is, change, will happen if we allow it to happen. This means giving up our pre-conceived ideas of what should be happening and trusting that if we pay attention to the "how" then all will be well. Learning often takes mysterious paths. And, to be sure, following the "how" might well not lead the pupil to the goal they originally thought they wanted to achieve, but to a different, perhaps more authentic one.

The Thinking Learner's Body: A Note about using the Explorations with your Students

Although I have written this book with the teacher in mind, students can, of course, also profit from it. The learner's body, like the teacher's, needs to be given an acknowledged place in education, and that does not just mean putting more physical exercise lessons on the timetable, however important these may be. Learning, like teaching and everything else we do, is a psycho-physical activity. We are, quite simply, mind and body. How we use our body affects our mind and vice versa. For this reason, the explorations in this book offer potential material for classroom use, whatever the subject being taught.

However, we need to be aware that for some students these explorations can be quite challenging. They might, for example, arouse the fear of loss of face. Or they might appear to be childish. For some students they may also run counter to cultural norms concerning status, authority, and the roles of teacher and student. It is important to proceed with sensitivity.

Above all, you need to give good rationales for why you are asking your students to do the explorations you choose and you need to emphasise how they can benefit from doing them. Which ones you choose, how you present them in class, how far you take them - these questions you, the teacher, are best placed to answer. You are the best judge of what might or might not work for your particular groups, classroom setting, institution, course content.

On the other hand, doing these explorations in class can work wonders for group dynamics and really bring students together. This has certainly been my experience. Many explorations offer a breath of fresh air and break with classroom conventions. Students often respond positively to that. Of course it is crucial that you, the teacher, have the courage of your convictions. You must be willing to demonstrate and go where angels fear to tread. And it helps to be able to laugh at yourself. In this as in most other aspects of teaching, how you present affects how your class will respond.

Centering: This is the most fundamental body-mind skill and the one which you might well introduce in class. You can, for example, present this by suggesting that being centered promotes calm alertness and makes people cleverer.

It can be practised standing or sitting (see explorations 9 and 11), and once it has become familiar need only take a few seconds. You can reduce the exploration to a few easily identifiable postural landmarks: feet and contact to the floor; sitting bones (if done sitting) and their contact to the chair; long spine, coming up to your full height with your head balancing freely; eyes looking out into the room.

Wider Classroom Applications

Presence: This is perhaps the most important quality for classroom success for both teacher and student. In addition to centering, sensory awareness explorations can promote presence.

Ask your students to notice:
where they have contact with any points of support (the floor, the chair, the desk)
their breathing
their clothing and its feel on the skin
air temperature
patterns of light and shade

Ask them to:
look into all four corners of the room
look up to the ceiling
notice who is sitting in the corners of their eyes
be aware of space all around them

You don't need to do all of these every time. One awareness exploration at the beginning of the lesson is usually enough. This can be done in a few seconds, just to get everyone mentally into the same space, namely the classroom. Alternatively, you can also integrate this into your lesson at any time, not just at the beginning. See also exploration 54.

Voicework: If you do student presentations or other tasks involving speaking in class, you can use them as a reason to introduce some voicework and presentation skills work. You can emphasise how the voice adds to (or detracts from) impact. Preface a lesson with a short body and voice warm-up (see chapter three). If you need to reduce the warm-up to the bare bones, focus on centering, hissing, and humming through the face.

Speaking Skills: Again, if speaking in class is important and valued, then use some of the explorations in chapter five to get your students more aware of what they can do with their speaking apparatus (jaw, lips, tongue). You will probably need to focus on activating. This needs to be done with sensitivity. Choose carefully how you present this. You need to build up to this by introducing your class to centering and basic voicework first. Be prepared to demonstrate yourself and for you all to have a laugh.

Listening Skills: The wide focus hearing exploration (exploration 36.3) can be useful for bringing your students' attention back into the classroom.

---

[1] Patsy M. Lightbown and Nina Spada, *How Languages are Learned* (Oxford University Press, Oxford, 2006), p.190. See also pp.77-82

[2] Thanks to Regina Nening-Dougan for her thoughts on this aspect.

9

THE ALEXANDER TECHNIQUE

For the Alexander Technique doesn't teach you something new to do. It teaches you how to ... deal with habit and change. (Frank Pierce Jones)

If you would like to discover more about how the principles underlying this book can help you, then you might like to take lessons from an Alexander Technique teacher, for much of what is presented in this book is inspired by the Alexander Technique.

The fundamental goal of every lesson in the Technique is to help you improve how you use your self. "The self" is the term coined by Frederick Matthias Alexander, the Technique's originator, for the human psycho-physical organism in its entirety. It encompasses the body with all its parts, organs, muscles, and it includes thoughts, beliefs, emotions, ideas, and the imagination. In short, it encompasses the whole human being. How you use yourself is how you respond, in your totality, to every situation of your life. In some situations you will respond in ways which promote your health and happiness and those of the people around you. In other situations you will not. In the former case you are using yourself well; in the latter you are using yourself less well. But in both cases, you are reacting with your whole being, with your self.

Our habits are usually our biggest obstacle to good use. And the most harmful habit we almost all have is that of end gaining, that is, of wanting to reach a goal regardless of what we do to ourselves in the process. Ends triumph over means, "what" triumphs over "how". As a result we often go through our daily lives heedless of our deeper needs, and moving against our own intrinsic structure and inherent functioning. We develop compensatory tensions which cause discomfort. As you have already explored in this book, the first and most important step to improving how you use yourself is to say "no" to those unhelpful habits of end gaining, to stop and go back to neutral.

Most Alexander Technique teachers work with a combination of gentle, non-manipulative manual guidance and verbal instruction. The Alexander Technique student is made aware of the habits which interfere with their natural functioning and cause compensatory, unnecessary tension. They are taught how to stop those unhelpful habits so that their natural functioning can be restored. Often everyday movements are used in order to learn and practise the main principles of the Technique. But of course the principles can be learnt, practised, and applied to anything of particular relevance to the student, from running and juggling to giving a presentation, handling a tricky negotiation, or managing difficult emotional issues. The student usually then discovers that improving how they do things improves the results they get.

The Technique is rooted in Alexander's investigation into his own habits surrounding the stimulus of public speaking and the discoveries he made as a result. It is based on his personal experience. It can therefore be illuminating to take a look at his story of discovery.

The Alexander Technique

Alexander's Story of Discovery

F.M. (as he liked to be called) Alexander was born in Tasmania in 1869 and as a young man took to a career as a stage recitor, a profession which has largely died out today, but before the days of easily available sound recordings was not that unusual. Reciting Shakespeare was apparently a particular favourite, again not unusually for the time and place. At first, all went well and Alexander seemed to be all set to have a relatively successful career. However, after a few years disaster struck: he suffered increasingly from hoarseness when performing. In accordance with medical advice Alexander rested his voice, using it as little as he possibly could when off-stage and things seemed to improve. However, as soon as he went on stage to recite, the hoarseness returned.

From this he deduced that the cause of his problem must be something he was doing while reciting, rather than any problem with his vocal apparatus as such. Although his doctor agreed with Alexander's deduction, he honestly admitted that he could not help his patient, as he had no idea what Alexander might be doing while reciting which would lead to these problems. It was this impasse which decided Alexander to embark on what turned out to be a long process of self-observation and discovery which led to what is now called the Alexander Technique.

Alexander set up a series of mirrors from which he could observe himself from every angle while speaking and reciting. "I was particularly struck by three things that I saw myself doing", he later wrote. "I saw that as soon as I started to recite, I tended to pull back the head, depress the larynx and suck in breath through the mouth in such a way as to produce a gasping sound".[1] He then noticed that he had the same patterns when speaking normally, but to a much lesser degree, which led him to believe that this set of habits was connected to his voice problems when reciting. But how could he change things? "After some months I found that when reciting I could not by direct means prevent the sucking in of breath or the depressing of the larynx, but that I could to some extent prevent the pulling back of the head."[2] In addition he noticed that when he succeeded in preventing the pulling back of his head, the sucking in of breath and the depressing of the larynx were also indirectly checked. This led to two important discoveries about human functioning.

Discovery: how we use ourselves affects how we function.

Discovery: preventing a pulling back of the head leads to an improvement in functioning.

From this he argued that by actively putting his head definitely forward (rather than just not pulling it back) he would be able to achieve even better results in his voice. However, he soon discovered that this was not the case, in fact quite the contrary, and thereby made two further important discoveries.

Discovery: direct intervention causes another kind of wrong.

Discovery: misuse of one part (in this case the head) causes misuse in others (in this case the vocal mechanism); the human body is one connected whole.

After much experimentation and self-observation he concluded that while reciting it was necessary for him to send his head up as well as forward, so that his stature could lengthen and widen. However, this turned out to be much harder than anticipated, for as soon as he decided to recite his old bad habits kicked in, despite all his best intentions. To make the whole process even more frustrating, he noticed that he often felt he was doing something which the mirror told him he was not, and vice versa.

Despite all these difficulties, Alexander had actually discovered three further foundation stones of human functioning.

Discovery: the neck needs to be released to allow the head to go forwards and up in order for the human body to function in an optimal way.

Discovery: our sensory perception is unreliable; we cannot assume that what we feel we are doing is actually what we are doing.

Discovery: we are very largely governed by habit; we almost invariably respond to stimuli in habitual and therefore unconscious ways.

After many failed attempts to speak while sending his head forward and up, Alexander decided that it would be necessary to refuse to react habitually in the first instance to the stimulus to speak.[3] After having refused to react in his habitual mode he gave himself his orders, but instead of trying actively to carry out the order he remained on the level of thinking alone. Thus he mentally sent (directed) his head forward and up. While speaking, he then continued to give his orders (directing thoughts) through all the critical moments when the habits wanted to kick in again.

Discovery: the key to change lies in refusing to react in our habitual manner to a stimulus which tends to put us wrong, and refreshing that refusal by sending ourselves appropriate directing thoughts while we perform the activity.

This is a mental activity, a new way of thinking the American philosopher and educationist John Dewey called "thinking in activity".[4]

Perhaps unsurprisingly, after all those years spent in self-observation and reflection, Alexander had lost interest in performing on stage and instead resolved to disseminate his discoveries. In 1904 he moved to London where he made quite a name for himself, particularly in the theatrical and literary worlds. Pupils included the actors Henry Irving, Viola Tree and Lily Brayton and the writers Aldous Huxley and George Bernard Shaw. While in London, Alexander founded a school which incorporated his work, trained the first group of Alexander Technique teachers, and spread his discoveries, particularly in the English-speaking world. He died in London in 1955.[5] Nowadays, the method named after him is a part of many performing arts trainings worldwide and is increasingly recognised and used in complementary medicine.

Applications
The Alexander Technique can be applied to anything we do, from the most mundane activities to the most specialised, from using a computer, driving a car, doing the washing-up to performing brain surgery, singing an opera aria or setting the next Olympic world record. It is recognised as a powerful tool for enhancing well-being and promoting skills by many professional groups.

Performing artists: The Technique's longest-established clientele is made up of performers who recognise its benefits in enhancing their performance skills and helping to prevent performance-related injuries. In many performing arts colleges the Technique has become a compulsory part of the curriculum for young performers of all kinds and styles: musicians, singers, actors, dancers, classically trained and not. Many famous names have learnt the Technique and swear by it. They include: John Cleese, Dame Judi Dench, Alan Rickman, Lenny Henry, Ralph Fiennes, Madonna, Sting, Dame Emma Kirkby, Sir Paul McCartney, Sir Colin Davis and many more.

Sportspeople have also long recognised the benefits of the Technique, for example American equestrian Sally Swift, British rower Matthew Pinsent and Canadian Olympic marathon runner Paul Collins, who went on to become a Alexander Technique teacher himself.

Public speakers: A growing number of radio and TV presenters, politicians, lecturers, business people, and public speakers of all kinds recognise how the Technique can help them meet the demands of their profession.

Medical practitioners: The benefits of the Technique are being increasingly recognised in the medical world and it is particularly recommended for back pain sufferers and those with conditions related to poor posture, mobility impairment and balance issues. The results of the first controlled clinical trial into the efficacy of the Technique for chronic lower back pain were published in the British Medical Journal on 19 August 2008. It showed that long-term benefits are derived from having lessons.

At the workplace: Many employers recognise the benefits of the Technique. It has been used by numerous companies, including the BBC, Chanel, Hewlett Packard, Victorinox, The Guardian, The British Library.

Children and young people are also increasingly being introduced to the Technique.[6]

However, at the moment many teachers, whether at primary, secondary or tertiary level, are not getting the help they deserve and that the Technique could offer them. The Alexander Technique does not yet have an established place in teacher training institutions or professional development programmes for teachers. I hope that this book has shown in a practical way how the principles of the Alexander Technique can enhance teachers' well-being and also their teaching skills. It can help teachers meet the various and often taxing demands of their profession and also make them better teachers. For the sakes of both teachers and students, it deserves to be part of every teacher training and development curriculum.

How to find an Alexander Technique Teacher
Worldwide, there are two main professional organisations for Alexander Technique teachers.

By far the larger is an umbrella organisation, Alexander Technique Affiliated Societies (ATAS), which brings together the national organisations of many countries. Represented countries so far include: Australia, Austria, Belgium, Brazil, Canada, Denmark, Finland, France, Germany, Israel, Netherlands, New Zealand, Norway, South Africa, Spain, Switzerland, UK (including Ireland), USA.
For the contact details of the affiliated society of the respective country, please see the ATAS website at www.alexandertechniqueworldwide.com. Follow the links to the website of the society for that country. There you can find a

list of the Alexander Technique teachers in that country who have completed the training recognised by ATAS.

For the United Kingdom (including Ireland) the affiliated society is The Society of Teachers of the Alexander Technique (STAT). Its website can be found at www.stat.org.uk.

The second, smaller, organisation is Alexander Technique International (ATI). Its website can be found at www.ati-net.com.

---

[1] F.M.Alexander, *The Use of the Self: Its Conscious Direction in Relation to Diagnosis, Functioning and Control of Reaction* (Gollancz, London, 1985), p.26. First published in 1932.
[2] Ibid., p.27
[3] Ibid., p.40
[4] Ibid., p.42
[5] For more about F.M.Alexander's life see Michael Bloch, *F.M.Alexander: The Life of Frederick Matthias Alexander Founder of the Alexander Technique* (Little, Brown, London, 2004)
[6] For more on this see, for example, Sue Holladay, *Playing with Posture: Positive Child Development using the Alexander Technique* (HITE, London, 2012)

www.ingramcontent.com/pod-product-compliance
Ingram Content Group UK Ltd.
Pitfield, Milton Keynes, MK11 3LW, UK
UKHW041957230426
12048UKWH00008B/388